MAKING ARCHITECTURE THROUGH BEING HUMAN

Architecture can seem complicated, mysterious or even ill-defined, especially to a student being introduced to architectural ideas for the first time. One way to approach architecture is simply as the design of human environments. When we consider architecture in this way, there is a good place to start – ourselves. Our engagement in our environment has shaped the way we think which we, in turn, use to then shape that environment. It is from this foundation that we produce meaning, make sense of our surroundings, structure relationships and even frame more complex and abstract ideas. This is the start of architectural design.

Making Architecture Through Being Human is a reference book that presents 51 concepts, notions, ideas and actions that are fundamental to human thinking and how we interpret the environment around us. The book focuses on the application of these ideas by architectural designers to produce meaningful spaces that make sense to people. Each idea is isolated for clarity in the manner of a dictionary with short and concise definitions, examples and illustrations. They are organized in five sections of increasing complexity or changing focus. While many of the entries might be familiar to the reader, they are presented here as instances of a larger system of human thinking rather than simply graphic or formal principles. The cognitive approach to these design ideas allows a designer to understand the greater context and application when aligned with their own purpose or intentions.

Philip D. Plowright is Professor of Architectural Design and Theory at Lawrence Technological University, USA. He is an academic researcher, theorist and licenced architect with degrees in studio art, architecture and cognitive linguistics. His interest focuses on developing clarity around foundational knowledge in the applied design disciplines for use in teaching and production environments. His previous book, *Revealing Architectural Design* (Routledge 2014), addressed the larger thinking frameworks that structure architectural design methods while his research monograph, *Qualitative Embodiment in English Architectural Discourse* (Universidad de Castilla-La Mancha 2017), looked at latent meaning found between people and environments based on conceptual metaphors and embodied knowledge.

MAKING ARCHITECTURE THROUGH BEING HUMAN
A Handbook of Design Ideas

Philip D. Plowright

Routledge
Taylor & Francis Group

LONDON AND NEW YORK

First published 2020
by Routledge
2 Park Square, Milton Park, Abingdon, Oxon OX14 4RN

and by Routledge
52 Vanderbilt Avenue, New York, NY 10017

Routledge is an imprint of the Taylor & Francis Group, an informa business

British Library Cataloguing-in-Publication Data
A catalogue record for this book is available from the British Library

Library of Congress Cataloging-in-Publication Data
Names: Plowright, Philip D., author.
Title: Making architecture through being human :
a handbook of design ideas / Philip D. Plowright.
Description: Abingdon, Oxon ; New York, NY : Routledge, 2020.
Identifiers: LCCN 2019039089 (print) | LCCN 2019039090 (ebook) |
ISBN 9780367204761 (hbk) | ISBN 9780367204778 (pbk) |
ISBN 9780429261718 (ebk)
Subjects: LCSH: Architectural design. | Architecture–Human factors.
Classification: LCC NA2750 .P585 2020 (print) |
LCC NA2750 (ebook) | DDC 721–dc23
LC record available at https://lccn.loc.gov/2019039089
LC ebook record available at https://lccn.loc.gov/2019039090

ISBN: 978-0-367-20476-1 (hbk)
ISBN: 978-0-367-20477-8 (pbk)
ISBN: 978-0-429-26171-8 (ebk)

Typeset in Myriad Pro
by Newgen Publishing UK

Printed in the United Kingdom
by Henry Ling Limited

TABLE OF CONTENTS

MAKING ARCHITECTURE THROUGH BEING HUMAN

WHAT THIS BOOK IS ABOUT

THIS IS A BOOK OF IDEAS that we use to make architecture. Some would restrict architecture to mean the design of a building as a sculptural object, and others might claim all design acts to be architectural from making movies to designing budgets. Still others use the term "architecture" to refer to the development of software or of foreign policy. In this book, architecture is the practice of designing human environments through the arrangement of form and voids to support human activity – with a stress on the "human" part of that statement. The ideas in the sections that follow are ones that people use to make sense of the spaces they inhabit – how we make a human environment meaningful for humans. These ideas are very basic but important because they form the foundation of more complex arrangements and intentions. As such, the point of view of the book is based on how we think, how we prioritize ideas, and how those ideas take physical shape in our world.

The basic design principles presented here are intended as a resource for beginning architectural design students. It is meant as a reference book or studio companion to be used in much the same way as a dictionary or glossary. None of the ideas in this book should be new – in fact, the best thing that can happen is if a reader finishes an entry and simply realises that they already knew the content presented but had not really considered the significance. What the book is meant to do is to bring clarity to the ideas, accessibility to the concepts and persistence to the terminology. When we all use the same word to mean the same thing, we have a much better ability to develop a deeper understanding of our chosen field of study and practice.

SEEING IS THINKING, MAKING IS THINKING

THIS BOOK STARTS WITH a very simple premise – the thinking processes we use to understand our environment are the same processes we use to design that environment. More than just this, those thinking processes are the same ones we use for everything. Although we have a long cultural tradition that separates our thinking into separate containers – visual thinking, emotional thinking, thinking through making, design thinking – these are not actually different thinking structures. They are simply terms we use to describe different sensory sources (sight or sound), different priorities (logic, emotions) or limiting our thinking to different tactics (making, exploration, empathy). We use these approaches to communicate our knowledge of the world to others as well as to ourselves – either through speech, text, drawing, model, or motion. Each mode priorities a different type of information and makes that information easier to access. The goal for humans is efficiency and frugality – our minds use an approach to processing information that will get us the best results in the fastest way using the least amount of energy. We can write a sculpture, draw a novel or act out a building but it would take more work and open up many more issues of misunderstanding. We might choose a less efficient approach to look at something, but this choice would be based on receiving some value that we could not get from the typical approach. However, none of this changes the underlying structure that we use to process that information – how our minds have developed through environmental pressures to work the way they do.

Another premise of the book is that our thinking is embodied. This means that we cannot separate how we think from our physical senses and bodily experience. In fact, our physical experiences provide the basic structure and meaning to our thoughts. We pay little attention to this knowledge but use it constantly to make sense of ourselves and our surroundings. We only have to consider some basic ideas to illustrate shared, embodied knowledge – just consider why we all assume that to be *high* or *up* is good; why to be *inside* is to be protected or to belong; why *sour* is used to describe things that become a negative experience even if it is not something we eat (such as people or relationships); why *brightness* is good, important, or the ability to think well; why *dark* is used for things that scare us or are ethically questionable; why we interchange the word *see* for the word *know*; and why we assume *forward* is the same as progress even though one is a direction and the other is a concept? While these examples are taken from spoken or written language, we use the same embodied knowledge to make sense of things we see, things we move through, things we make and many of our basic values. The cognitive functions developed in concrete, physical experiences are shared between speech, abstract thought, conceptualization, imagination and visualization. This is a very good thing as it means that people have a vast amount of shared knowledge that starts with the same experiences – the interaction of our body in an environment.

For an architectural designer, this turns out to be important. It means that making something and what something means are intimately related. Our environment influences the way we think and how we think affects what we put into the environment. It is this relationship that provides the foundation for understanding to occur between the designer who makes an artefact (object or environment) and those who use that artefact.

SYSTEMS AND UNCERTAINTY

OUR BUILT ENVIRONMENT IS a complex, dynamic system. A system is a collection of things that work together to create a whole. It is complex because the whole cannot be predicted by simply adding up the properties of the parts. Dynamic means that the relationships within the system are always changing, which makes it difficult to predict fixed outcomes. It is easy to think about buildings, built forms and their arrangement as a system as they are clearly made up of many identifiable parts aligned with a whole. It is much more difficult to consider them as dynamic as they are obviously static – we think about our buildings as inert and isolated objects. They do not move and, in general, they do not respond to environmental forces by changing the relationship between parts once constructed. The objects of our built environment are made of hard, durable materials – concrete, steel, glass, brick and wood. None of these materials have dynamic properties as part of their nature. So, what makes our environment a complex, dynamic system? People.

Architecture arranges surfaces in space to be used by people, and people are not static. They move, make choices, have moods, form relationships, generate memories, change their focus and get distracted. Our surrounding environment also changes constantly and at different scales – the sun moves behind a cloud, a storm blows in, day turns to night, seasons change, materials decay and temperatures fluctuate. The weather can affect our mood and our comfort. We might rush through the rain at one point and not really pay attention to our surroundings. We might then come through the same environment on a warm day, choose a longer route and see things we missed before. Each condition (surfaces, textures, light conditions, path, mood, memory, etc.) is a variable in a larger system. The relationship between variables will change slightly with people introducing different points-of-view, orientations and states-of-mind making a single, fixed and repeatable experience very difficult. However, when we design in a human context, we should be more interested in *probability* than fixed absolutes. This means we chose to design for things that are likely to happen rather than attempting to design for something that will happen every time and always. In our built environment, the simplest building blocks of probabilities are based on embodied concepts that are formed by our relationship with our world. We use these as a basis to understand more complex things – either concrete or abstract.

The entries in this book are not a set of rules, they are a set of potentials. They describe a common foundation that underlies how humans understand their environment and how we project meaning into forms through the way our environment has shaped our thinking. These concepts, notions, ideas and actions have been isolated for clarity but this is never how they will be experienced in reality. Instead, our environments are complex, dynamic systems, and most spaces include all the ideas at the same time. There are also many variations, some exceptions and even a few contradictions as context and relative positioning changes meaning. Big, for example, usually means that we should pay attention or that something is important. However, when something is very, very big, the opposite happens – we ignore it. When big is combined with proximity, implied motion, imbalance, front and repetition, the normal interpretation of "pay attention" can be suppressed or extenuated. This is because meaning is related to real and specific situations – we require not just some symbol, form or word but also the context in which it is used in order to interpret it successfully.

HOW TO USE THIS BOOK

THIS BOOK IS INTENDED as a reference for fundamental ideas found in architectural design. It is similar to the model of a dictionary or glossary which presents each idea as simply and clearly as possible. This is done to make those ideas useful and the book should be approached in this spirit. It is not intended to be authoritative, rigid or even stand on its own. It is also not intended to claim to be the only way to design architecture. Rather, the book brings awareness to a type of information that is useful if we believe architecture has some relationship with humans and we care about relevance. This also means that the content presented here should be tested, challenged, adapted and expanded through your own practice. None of the information in the book is new. The embodied ideas are well understood by disciplines in the cognitive sciences such as cognitive linguistics, cognitive psychology and cognitive anthropology but have little presence in architecture. Most of the entries in the first section, Formal Concepts, are listed on websites and introductory books on graphic design and interaction design but are treated as formal rather than cognitive events (i.e. cognitive refers to intellectual activity or mental processes). The book gathers these ideas and presents them as part of a larger structure that is grounded in human thinking and highly relevant to architectural design.

As a glossary, this book is not intended to be read linearly from beginning to end – although this is acceptable and may work well for many readers. Sections are used to group entries based on increasing complexity or a change in focus but the entries in those sections are simply arranged alphabetically. This is done to suppress interpreting any larger hierarchical or epistemological relationship by the order of entries where none exists. *Centrality* is before *Orientation* simply because "C" is before "O" in the alphabet. This book should be understood as systematic rather than linear. Most readers may prefer to select a topic and continue to related sections using the several references listed in each entry to the other ideas found in the book. None of the ideas in this book stand by themselves and the references are there to make sure that the connections between ideas are explicit and accessible to a reader.

While architecture tends to focus on objects, most of the content of this book is about the relationship between space, the surfaces that define it and ourselves. The illustrations are deliberately simplistic and use primary forms of planes, cubes, orthotopes, cylinders and spheres. Human bodies are not represented but always implied through a point-of-view. This is to connect the drawings as clearly as possible to the ideas. It also allows the forms to be considered at multiple scales – a group of cubes grouped to suggest a relationship through proximity might be districts in a city, several buildings in a district, kiosks on a street, objects at the scale of furniture or a raised pattern on a wall. The ideas in this book are independent of scale *while they stay in our heads*. It is only when we apply them to a context does scale have an effect. Any of the ideas might be found from the very small to the very large as well as repeated several times at multiple scales in the same context – the creation of a container through the arrangement of furniture which is inside the container created by walls, inside the container created by building form, inside the container of a neighbourhood, and so on. Again, this is something to pay attention to in your own practice of architectural design. One thing to remember is our body is the reference point for all of our experiences, so this becomes the scale from which we understand the world.

MAKING ARCHITECTURE THROUGH BEING HUMAN

FORMAL CONCEPTS

WE UNDERSTAND OUR ENVIRONMENT from values that come from the experience of our bodies. This type of information is called *embodied* as it develops through our presence in a specific environment without us being consciously aware. In architectural design, embodied concepts are grounded in three aspects: our body position and orientation, our ability to move and the way our vision prioritizes certain aspects of our visual field. This embodied knowledge is the foundation of how we extract meaning from our surroundings and how we build more complex ideas.

Our bodies are our centre from which our senses extend outwards. We have an orientation that is defined through the location of our sense organs, the jointing of our appendages and gravity – this gives us a front, back, sides, top and bottom. We can move and when we move, we prioritize forward over other directions. We do not tend to move randomly but instead we decide on a destination and look for paths to reach that goal. Our sense of vision is biased as it has developed to identify things that matter quickly. We prioritize things that are understood as objects, things that move, things that contrast with their surroundings, things that are big or close and we group objects together in order to make larger patterns (which allows us to expend less energy). This embodied knowledge is the basis of a set of formal concepts that place an understandable logic onto our environment. They allow us to introduce a formal order that is recognizably human.

The entries in this section address these basic concepts. Their importance is not as isolated ideas but as a foundation for more complex notions, ideas and actions in constructing environments.

ALIGNMENT

ALIGNMENT MEANS THAT things are arranged along an imaginary line. Imaginary lines are used in other concepts as well (see *Axis* and *Radiosity*) but in alignment, the line reinforces the idea of edge. An edge in architectural design is defined by our visual field and we interpret alignment based on what we see in the normal human field of view. This prioritizes the relationship between outer surfaces of visible objects rather than any other aspect, such as interpreted centre of mass. Alignments in the built environment generally involve building façades (façade is a French word used in architectural design and means "face" or principle side), walls, doors, windows, parapets, ceiling heights and columns. The alignment of these elements supports architectural ideas that scale from the small to the very large – from the placement of openings in a façade to the organization of city blocks. In all cases, alignment allows for coherence between parts as it produces a clearly understandable and simple organization (see *Coherence*).

Alignment is part of pattern finding (see *Pattern*) and used to support ordering principles (see *Axis*, *Centrality* and *Radiosity*). If we see a row of buildings and their façades align to create a visual edge, we can understand them as a group of buildings rather than individual objects. We know the edge that they all reinforce is important and creates an understanding of order for that environment. We expect the edges on the alignment to be important in some way with some difference of quality, activity or experience between one side of the edge and the other. Aligned edges in a visual field are also more likely

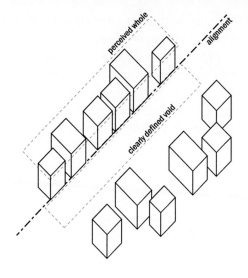

Alignment: Defining PART-TO-WHOLE Relationships

to be fronts and clearly define the relationship between negative and positive spaces (see *Solid-Void*). For example, if we have a series of building façades that align, they more clearly define an edge which makes the adjacent void, which is the street, more defined and, thus, more understandable (see *Containment*). The most important role for alignment is the construction of a relationship between elements in the environment (see *Relationship*). By bringing one or more aspects of an object into alignment though an imaginary line, we create a natural association between those two or more things.

While a large part of alignment is about human satisfaction based on visual composition, the imaginary lines created by things aligning can relate to other types of information in our environment. Windows aligning, for example, might make the internal organization of the building more understandable by projecting the internal layout of floors onto the outer surface of the building. Buildings can be associated with each other through alignment to define horizontal datums in the urban context (a datum is a reference line or plane from which other things can be measured – such as sea level or floor elevation). Alignments do not have to be complete for us to understand them. We can also have several different alignments within one space and these might include horizontal alignments, vertical alignments and alignments at multiple scales. We will separate these various alignments into individual relationships automatically, creating a more complex and layered space that is still clearly understandable. Each alignment can mean something different depending on its association. Some might define solid-void relationships, some create larger composite objects out of smaller elements, some imply path for movement, some create balance or harmony through proportions and some suggest types of activities, occupations or other human needs.

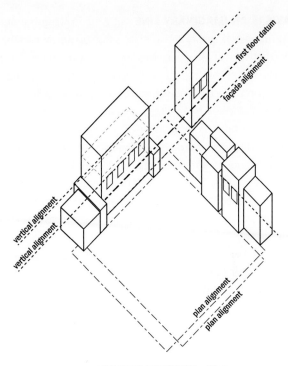

Alignment: CONTEXTUAL EXPRESSION and Datum

AXIS

AN AXIS IS AN IMAGINARY LINE – it is not a thing but an idea. People use this imaginary line to make sense of objects and the relationship between objects, ourselves and our environment. One definition for an axis comes from physics – it is a line that projects from the centre around which an object rotates. However, architecture does not generally include real motion or rotation, so a more useful definition of axis comes from geometry. That definition presents an axis as generated by how we perceive objects. One way we understand objects is through imagining a line that either extends from, or passes through, the centre of mass for each of the major spatial dimensions of the object. That line, as a projected extension of the object, allows us to associate that object with other objects and ideas. The idea that an axis creates an association or organizes relationships means that it cannot simply be considered as a value-free line. While the major spatial dimensions are the basic cartesian coordinates of X (length), Y (width) and Z (height), an architectural designer will make decisions about which of these are more important depending on context. This means that when we have more than one axis present in an environment, there will often be different levels of importance between them (see *Hierarchy*). In this way, an axis might be considered either primary, secondary and tertiary in relation to other axes and the overall context.

The object from which an axis is formed does not need to be a *literal* object but any aspect of the environment that can be bounded. This might include voids like a street, path, room or corridor. In all these cases the axis is generated by interpreting the centre of mass

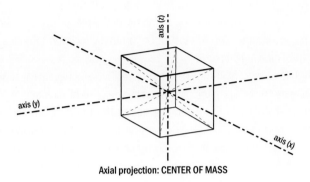

Axial projection: CENTER OF MASS

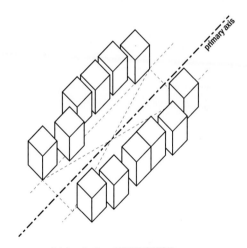

Axial projection: CENTER OF VOID

of the defined void. Once we understand the idea of the axis, we no longer need an object to exist before the axis. Rather, we can use the idea of the axis to organize space and direct the placement of objects in that environment. In this way, it becomes a very important idea as a part of *ordering principles*.

While an axis might not be real, it is really useful because it allows architects to set up relationships, create a sense of direction, imply motion and place order into environments. The introduction of an axis in the design process, or the perception of one in the environment, makes that environment more comprehensible. As a single line, an axis defining a void, series of solids or relationship between elements creates the *linear ordering principle*. In an architectural environment, this often manifests as a straight corridor, path, circulation spine or some other linear organizational structure that arranges events, spaces, objects along this line. When a linear ordering principle is used, the starting and ending locations often have special significance. Two axes placed perpendicular to each other, so there is a point where they cross, create an *intersectional ordering principle*. An intersection is often used as a circulation strategy or to bring attention to an important part of the environment as it creates a focal point where the axes cross (see *Importance* and *Hierarchy*). Several axes placed perpendicular to each other in parallel rows creates a *grid ordering principle*. While a grid involves several intersections, when intersections are similar and repeated it creates a field rather than a focus (see *Repetition*). Grid systems are used to bring equality and regularity into a larger environment.

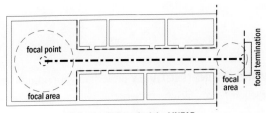

Axis as ordering principle: LINEAR

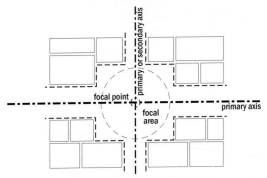

Axis as ordering principle: INTERSECTION

Axis as ordering principle: GRID

BALANCE

AS HUMANS, WE INSTINCTIVELY understand our position in space, what direction we are facing and whether we are upright or not. This knowledge comes from our body through embodied experiences generated by basic senses and motor functions (sight, equilibrium, touch, somatosensory, proprioception, etc.). Our body provides us with notions of centre and wholeness as well as balance. These ideas are important to us but as embodied knowledge, we are not actively aware of the influence they have on many of the values we hold. In the case of balance, our personal body experience through our spine and posture makes the notions of *up* and *vertical* into positive conditions; our experience in our environment makes *firmness* and *stability* important as acts of resisting gravity, of not falling over, of avoiding injury, and to have control over our existence; and our social values consider *erectness* as positive, aligning with ideas of justice and ethics (as in, to be upright is to be just).

Gravity, one of the factors that makes balance necessary, is so persistent that we often forget that it is a serious force in our lives. We are very good at estimating the effect of gravity on objects in the world, and those objects include ourselves and other people. We can know something has the potential to fall before it falls (see *Implied Stability*). We estimate weight from visual clues and understand shapes that project a sense of stability. A form that is thicker at the bottom appears more stable to us, while a large mass on a single, thin support placed off-centre appears precarious. It turns out that balance is a goal that allows us to make sense of life and we extend this concept from the

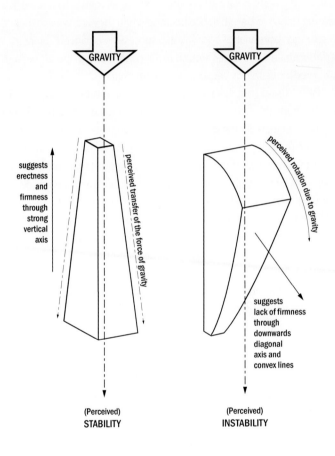

suggests erectness and firmness through strong vertical axis

perceived transfer of the force of gravity

perceived rotation due to gravity

suggests lack of firmness through downwards diagonal axis and convex lines

GRAVITY

GRAVITY

(Perceived)
STABILITY

(Perceived)
INSTABILITY

physical experience of gravity and our own body's orientation to how we understand our built environment. Balanced compositions, balanced effects, balanced priorities – these all matter to people. We expect things to be in balance because when they are, we experience a stronger potential of survival and success as balanced things can endure against the forces around us. Of course, being human, we also like precarious things because they seem exciting.

People seek out balance in compositional arrangements – for architecture, the priority is the relationship between the left and right sides of objects in the environment, although we also understand balance through up and down as well as inside and outside. While this might suggest that things need to be symmetrical through the same elements facing each other across a centre vertical axis, it is not necessary. We have the ability to interpret compositional balance in several different ways – strict symmetry is just the most obvious. Asymmetrical balance works through creating a sense of equal weight on both sides of an axis but without duplicating the same forms or elements. As long as each side is considered to contain the same amount of visual mass, then balance is achieved. The sides do not even need to contain the same volume, nor the axis be in the centre. Part-to-whole balance works through several small elements equalling the perceived mass or weight of one larger element. The small elements are understood as grouped into a perceived whole through thinking actions such as similarity (see *Relationship* and *Containment*). The overall effect can be either symmetrically or asymmetrically arranged.

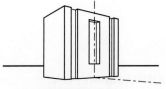

SYMMETRICAL Balance

ASYMMETRICAL Balance (Centre Axis)

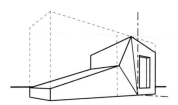

ASYMMETRICAL Balance (Offset Axis)

PART-TO-WHOLE Balance

CENTRALITY

CENTRALITY IS AN IMAGINARY POINT that gathers space around it and creates a perceived circle. The circle marks an area of influence where things can be at the centre of the circle, within the circle, at the periphery of the circle or outside the circle. Each of these locations has a different meaning for us. While we use centrality as a way to interpret our environment, the idea comes from our own body and our sensory experience of the world. Our bodies hold a central and dominate position in the experience of our environment – literally. This is because we understand the world through information gathered by our senses and those senses are gathered together at one physical location. Our body is the point from which all experience starts and from which we each, as individuals, project outwards to affect our world. The reach of our senses introduces the idea of distance and effect. We understand that things that are close to our bodies can interact with us; we can reach out, grasp, hold, touch or be touched. We also know that things farther away are maybe something we do not need to think about at the moment so are not as important (see *Proximity* and *Relationship*). This understanding creates the idea of centrality.

Architecture uses centrality as one of several ordering principles, either by itself or in conjunction with axis to make other, more complex ordering principles (see *Radiosity*). This is because centrality allows us to make sense of our environment by defining clear relationships in the same way as other ordering principles, such as linear, intersection and grid (see *Axis*). While an axial-based ordering system uses direction or intersection to define relationships, a *central ordering principle*

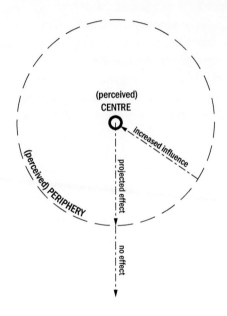

uses distance away from a perceived centre to generate meaning. Centrality is a basic gradient where a location that is closer to the centre is considered more influential or important, and a location further away is considered less important. The peripheral is the farthest zone of influence that the centre might have on the surrounding area and beyond this threshold, there is no relationship or effect.

In formal environments, centrality can be created in one of three ways. The first is the creation of a strong centre with a weak edge. An easy way to accomplish this is to place an object in an open space. This might be an entire building or some smaller element such as a fountain, kiosk, monument or grouping of furniture. The object becomes a focal point and projects its influence outwards to imply a circle of effect. The second is a weak centre with a strong edge. When people experience a clear boundary that encircles a space, we naturally associate a centre point with the boundary even if that centre is not marked. We experience this in urban squares and public gathering spaces. It is important that the space tends towards a convex space (see *Convexity*) as any sense of directionality will produce an axis instead of a centre. Convexity does not necessarily mean a circle but any shape defined by a series of points that have visibility to all other points in that volume. The most common convex shape in our built environment is a square but even an irregular shape can create convexity and then centrality. The third way to produce centrality is with a centre and edge in balance. In this case, neither of the two elements need to be dominant as they work together to produce the ordering principle.

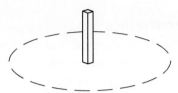

Strong Centre – Weak Edge

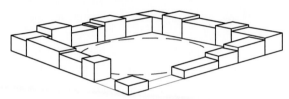

Weak Centre – Strong Edge

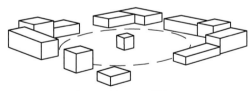

Balanced Centre and Edge

DIFFERENCE

IT IS THROUGH DIFFERENCE that we organize our priorities in the world. Where similarity makes relationships and builds associations through like-to-like comparisons (see *Similarity*), difference uses contrast to isolate a thing or an aspect from its surroundings. We could say that while similarity creates a field, difference creates an object. When we identify something that is different, it means that we should *pay attention*. This event identifies that thing as meaningful by *not being the same*, although we would still have to determine the nature of that meaning.

In architectural design, difference is created using contrast in visual information – we look for something dissimilar to those things around it. This is accomplished in several ways. When an attribute of an object significantly contrasts with the same attribute of things around it, the object related to those attributes is isolated in our minds. Formal attributes are things such as shape, size, material, texture and colour. Significant, in this case, is a contextual idea and can only be determined by considering the larger system and all of its elements. A change of scale might be significant in one context (i.e. meaningful because it creates difference) but insignificant in another (i.e. not meaningful as it does not create difference). For example, we might have a row of small buildings with one building that is larger. If the context surrounding the row contains other buildings that are also small, the larger one will stand out. However, if the context surrounding the row contains some larger buildings, then the presence of a large building in the row will not matter much due to a lack of contrast. Difference can also

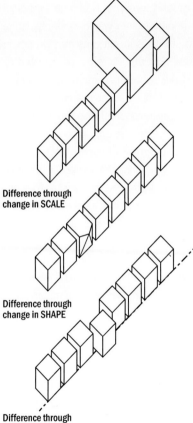

Difference through
change in SCALE

Difference through
change in SHAPE

Difference through
BREAKING PATTERN (alignment)

be produced by a contrast in environmental qualities such as light levels, acoustic properties or topography. An area that is significantly brighter than another, an area where sound is suddenly eliminated, or a change of ground level that is unique to the surroundings will all draw our attention. Another way we identify difference is through changes, gaps or conflicts in patterns that we perceive in the built environment (see *Pattern*). Patterns are powerful organizational structures for people, so when something does not fit a pattern, it draws our attention as much as the pattern itself.

When difference is introduced into the environment for effect, it does not have to be extreme, only recognizable. Environments are complex, dynamic systems and each object can be understood in multiple ways (see *Dimensionality*). While it is possible to create difference with a single attribute, it is also possible to align several properties and effects together to reinforce the idea (see *Coherence*). As such, difference might occur through any (or all) of these factors depending on the surrounding context.

As applied to architecture, difference is very useful. It is involved in all aspects of formal decision-making from identifying objects to be used as focal points, destinations or orientation elements. It is used as a part of ordering systems (a centre in *Centrality* can be made identifiable as a point of difference) and can also purposefully break an ordering system. When things are aligned to an edge, the intentional placement of something *not* on that edge breaks the pattern and produces difference which, in turn, draws our attention. Difference can be used to indicate that an object is important and then used as a focal element or to broadcast cultural information (i.e. "this building matters"). People are very good at sorting aspects of their environment through acts of grouping, organizing and associations to make sense of things. When we find something that does not fit, it matters to us.

FRONT

PEOPLE GIVE AN ORIENTATION and a sense of direction to things with which they interact – whether objects, ideas, events or emotions (see *Orientation* and *Directionality*). This does not mean that those things really have either an orientation or directionality, only that people think they do. One of the most important directions in orientation is *front* or *forward* as this is, for humans, the direction of interaction, engagement and access to knowledge of the world. Fronts are the location of our face – which means it is from this plane that we can see, speak and eat. The face also holds a large amount of information for social interaction which is important for us to maintain relationships with other people. Our limbs are jointed to make front the direction of action so that we may carry out various tasks and indicates the direction of movement.

It is important for us to find fronts in things that are not people so we can understand them and know how to relate ourselves to that object. To do this, we use the same knowledge of human interaction to understand things that are not human, projecting our values into our environment to understand it. Since humans have fronts as our plane of engagement, we expect that other things will also engage the world through their fronts. We determine what is the front of an object based on our interpretation of that object's formal composition. We use visual information to find something distinct or different in one location or plane when compared to the others. There is no strict rule to how this works as it can take many forms, be inferred in many ways and be located on (mostly) any plane or aspect. There are, however, some *probabilities* to how we understand front that are based on our own experience with our own bodies and other humans.

In architectural forms, we identify a front as the plane of a thing or object that is different to the others. Our eyes, noses, mouths, hands, sexual organs and toes are all found on the front of our bodies which creates more formal detail on this plane to any other (i.e. smaller, finer and more expressive elements are found there). Thus, we expect that when we find more detail in one plane of an object than another, that should be a front. We can also identify front through a change in material or shape that creates a difference or a highlight, where one side of the thing is different in some way to the others. People will naturally identify this difference and, by doing so, orient the object by assigning one plane as being more important than the rest. Another way front is determined is through the identification of anthropomorphic forms, such as things that suggest a full face, eyes, nose, mouth, arms or some other aspect of a human body. When a pattern of voids on a façade evokes a mouth or suggests a face, this allows us to orientate that form. The suggestion does not have to be very literal – even the most abstract suggestion of a face or body can be recognized. In all these cases, the front is the plane that is more detailed or different in some way and when we find a plane that is unarticulated lacking detail, activity or points of engagement, we will consider it as the back – and dismiss it as important. Fronts are usually located on a plane that is vertical, upright and accessible. This is especially true as the object gets bigger as we expect to be able to engage with fronts so we can interact with them easily (i.e. we don't naturally fly). A top *could* be interpreted as a front in certain situations if it was accessible in the visual field and had a clear path of movement to it. Once we assign front, the other major directions naturally follow.

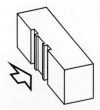

Front identified through added DETAIL

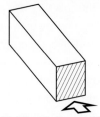

Front identified through change in TEXTURE

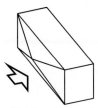

Front identified through change in SHAPE

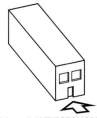

Front identified through ANTHROPOMORPHIC form

OBJECT-GROUND

WHEN WE ENGAGE the environment around us, we separate things considered to be objects from those things considered to be ground (in two-dimensional work, the *object* is called a *figure* while *ground* is also called *field*). Object and ground are both aspects of the same physical environment, but they are different conceptually. Objects are elements that can be separated from their surroundings and are distinct – that is, they are understood as not-the-same as their surroundings. This is a basic application of using difference to make distinctness (see *Difference*). Objects are things to which we pay attention and should consider in some way. Ground is everything around that object that produces the context in which it exists and is mostly ignored (i.e. is *background*). Ground is often produced through similarity, sameness and a sense of continuity (see *Similarity*). Neither object or ground are predetermined but, rather, we assign priority to what is an object and what is ground by our attention. This is defined through real or perceived edges and boundaries but also context and need (see *Objectification* and *Containment*). The purpose for deciding which things are objects and which are ground is due to the need to limit the amount of thinking we must do in any situation. If you paid attention to all aspects of the environment at the same level of focus, you would simply never move again or not be able to sort things that were important (i.e. the big bear with sharp teeth) from those things that are not as important (i.e. the line of trees in which the big bear is standing). Or, you might be able to sort out priorities but not fast enough to matter (i.e. the bear is no longer in the trees and you are inside the bear).

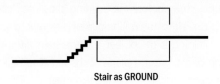

Stair as GROUND

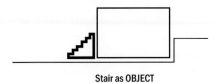

Stair as OBJECT

We can consider how things in architecture can be designed as object or ground by considering the example of a building with a stair or a ramp. Stairs and ramps are good examples of elements that may be either object or ground, depending on the immediate needs of the designer or a person who actually encounters the element. There are many examples of courthouses, opera houses and public museums in which the public street before the building "slips into", "rises through", "folds up" or "pushes into" the building itself (see *Implied Action*). In this example, the building is the object and the stairs are interpreted as a continuation of the ground plane of the city. The building is seen to "sit" on the stairs and, hierarchically, this means it is of a higher priority. However, stairs can also be designed as an object. In these cases, we would understand the stair and the building to be two separate things of more equal importance even if physically joined. As separate entities, we would assign them a relationship based on their formal composition. That relationship might be described using such terms as "touch", "brush", "penetrate" or "puncture" as we interpret their interaction based on distinctness. The words are different for object-to-object relationships rather than object-to-ground relationships because the conceptual understanding is different.

Once we have made an element or event in the environment discrete and separated it from ground, it allows us to consider it, manipulate it, act upon it, and, most importantly, put it into relationship with other things also considered to be objects. When we consciously decide to design some aspect of the environment as an object, it *changes the conceptual hierarchy of that environment*. This means the things that are present will be paid attention to in a different order and when we change that order, we change the way we understand that environment (see *Hierarchy*).

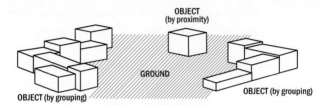

NEGATIVE SPACE as Ground

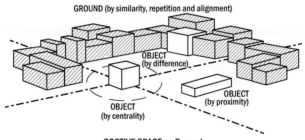

POSTIVE SPACE as Ground

OBJECTIFICATION

PEOPLE CONSTANTLY MAKE THINGS that are not objects into objects. Just think for a moment about how we describe ideas, intellectual positions, beliefs and emotions. You "bottle up your rage" or "give your love to someone" as if these intangible bodily experiences where either a physical substance (anger) or an object that could be passed hand to hand (love). As we understand our world through our embodied experiences, it is natural for us to make things we cannot touch into things we can as manipulating them in our minds is one way we understand and communicate it to others.

It is not just emotions and ideas that we make into physical things in order to understand and communicate, we also treat intangible phenomena in the physical environment in the same way. This is important for architecture as it is one of the ways we use environmental and social information to make formal design decisions (see *Asset-Constraint*). Phenomena might be human events such as movement, human social interactions such as crime or privacy, environmental factors such as light or airflow, or conceptual ideas such as emptiness or space. Any idea or event that can be conceptually bounded by considering its edges and area of effect can be made into an object or substance.

An object has a fixed form with uniform properties, well-defined boundaries, volume and mass. A substance can be understood as a variation of an object but where an object is fixed, a substance is physical matter that has uniform properties but a changeable form and predictable actions. Water, oil, wax, foam and powder are all

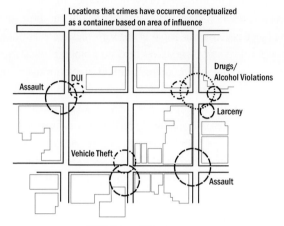

CRIME as an Object

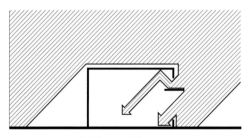

LIGHT as an Object

substances – they have persistent and uniform properties but their shapes can change depending on their context. The difference between whether the idea or event becomes an object or substance depends on its nature. For example, sunlight can be considered as an object because the angle of the sun's rays is consistent and fixed. Sunlight does not bend, swirl or distort around objects – it simply moves in a straight line unless blocked. Human movement, in contrast, is more useful if considered as a substance as while the event is consistent (including modes such as walking, cycling, driving or public transport), it is shaped by objects in the environment. As such, the movement of people – known as *circulation* – is often conceived as water or some other fluid. This is useful when considering human movement as a larger system and by looking at things that change the "flow" of movement like attractors, blockages and visible paths. By making the idea of movement into a substance, the architect can abandon the single instance of the human body as wilful and unpredictable to instead focus on more predictable habits of movement patterns.

Once we consider non-physical ideas and events as objects and substances, we can make physical form respond to these conceptual ideas using compositional techniques such as carving, attraction, addition, pressure, penetration, intersection and other dynamic forces. We do have to be careful of a type of fixedness that comes with objectification. Once we translate an idea or event into an object or substance, we tend to forget about the complexities of the original source. A stair or building as an object is often not thought of as integrated into the surrounding context; human movement as a substance can suppress the actions of individuals. While making ideas, events and other physical elements into objects and substances, we need to remind ourselves constantly of the goals and priorities of human environments.

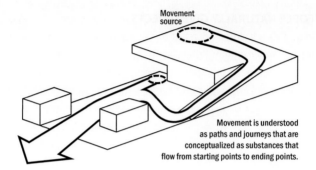

Movement
source

Movement is understood
as paths and journeys that are
conceptualized as substances that
flow from starting points to ending points.

MOVEMENT as a Substance

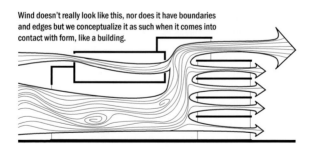

Wind doesn't really look like this, nor does it have boundaries
and edges but we conceptualize it as such when it comes into
contact with form, like a building.

WIND as a Substance

ORIENTATION

PEOPLE NATURALLY GIVE OBJECTS in the environment an orientation. This is a simple idea but has profound effect on how we interpret our environment. We give things an orientation because we, ourselves, have an orientation – we think in terms of things having tops and bottoms, fronts and backs, lefts and rights. Why? The basis of our understanding of our environment is formed from the experience of our bodies with gravity and fixed locations for our senses and appendages. We have heads at the top and feet at the bottom, we have a face on one side which creates a direction of front (see *Front*), we have symmetrical arms at our sides and stand upright. Since we can only, and have only, experienced the world from the point of view of our bodies, our bodies naturally shape the way we think and how we interpret our environment. Orientation is one of the most basic spatial ideas that originates from our bodies; we then use this knowledge to interpret other things in the environment because we tend to interpret other things *as being like us*. This means that when we consider things in our environment, we also give them tops and bottoms, fronts and backs, faces, heads and feet as well as lefts and rights – even if they do not really have them. The mapping of human values onto nonhuman things helps us know how to interact with those things. This might seem obvious, but it is so obvious that we never talk about it and rarely acknowledge the importance of it.

While we project orientations onto parts of our environment, we do not treat all directions as equal. This is because as part of human thinking, people consider different directions as having different

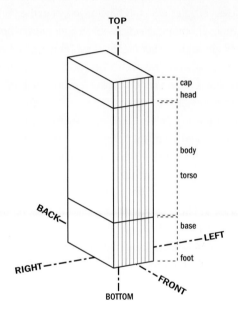

Standard Orientations

values. Orientation for humans works through three primary lines that we imagine pass through our centre of mass (see *Axis*). Each of these three lines ends in one of our primary directions creating the standard couples of up–down, front–back, and left–right. One end of each line is generally considered more positive than the other, so we find right prioritized over left, although this has little effect in the built environment. The more important directions for architecture are *up* and *front*. Up is generally considered better than down, as it has to do with intellect, social status and positive events. Up also relates to expressions of control and allows for vista and visibility – events that are important socially and emotionally for humans. Down, on the other hand, is generally a negative event and but can be used to suggest things that are protected, mysterious or unknown. Front is much more important than back as it relates to the ability to see, to understand, the ability to move, ideas of progress and to be in a better place than we are now (see *Directionality*). None of the six primary directions of up, down, left, right, back and front could exist if it was not for something else – centre. Without a centre, these directions do not make any sense (see *Centrality*). We unconsciously monitor our orientation in the world and if we sense an imbalance, eccentricity or directional ambiguity, we become conscious and attempt to correct that anomaly in some way. Much of architecture is making sure humans feel appropriately oriented (i.e. centred) in the world.

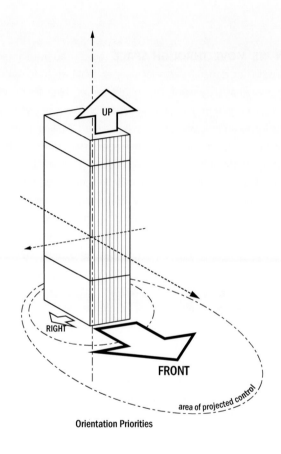

Orientation Priorities

PATH-GOAL

WHEN WE MOVE THROUGH SPACE, we do so with intention. Humans do not, generally, wander aimlessly but instead look for ways to achieve what they want. This might be reaching for an object, achieving recognition or arriving at a location. We conceive what we want as a *goal* and the way to get to it as a *path*. While a goal is a destination, a path is a trajectory through space that marks the forward motion of a body, object or entity. The idea of goals and paths comes from developing as a human in an environment. We understand that a moving object has a trajectory – an imaginary line that extends forward in the direction of movement and behind to trace where it has been. Humans are also objects that move through space. Our own movement is both physical and conceptual. Our bodies move in space following a line that our minds have mapped out to achieve where we wish to go. We leave a trail behind us of the memories of those places we have been. The combination of where we are going and where we have been creates a path. We look for paths by paying attention to certain environmental clues to help us navigate our environment and interact successfully with things in it – in other words, to get what we want. For architecture, a path is an indication that movement is possible while a goal is a location in space where things happen and the arrival at a destination.

We look to our built environment to allow us to recognize the location of our goals and to map a path of movement to achieve them. Goals do not have to be significant in order to make a path, nor do they always have to be clear or immediately visible. However, once

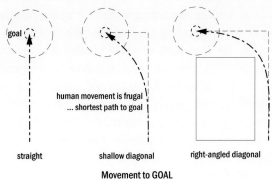

goal

human movement is frugal
... shortest path to goal

straight   shallow diagonal   right-angled diagonal

Movement to GOAL

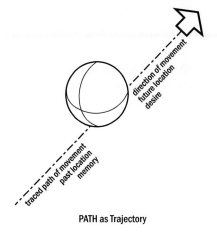

direction of movement
future location
desire

traced path of movement
past location
memory

PATH as Trajectory

engaged, there should be clues in the environment which makes the achievement of that goal possible. A goal could be as small as "I need to leave this room", "can we find a spot to talk?" or "where is the bathroom?". Our environment can also suggest goals that we did not know we had. Any aspect of the built environment has the potential of becoming a goal if, for example, it is contrasted with its surroundings (see *Difference*), terminates an axis (see *Axis*) or made important through a change in scale or luminosity (see *Importance*). These actions broadcast that we should pay attention to something that occurs at that place, and maybe something we should go have a look at. Once a goal is identified, we naturally start to look for a path.

Since the idea of a path includes the motion of the human body, it naturally involves the notion of time. Time, in turn, introduces the ideas of spatial sequences and shifting perspective – this simply means that people move through the environment as a series of connected experiences and each step a person takes changes the view of the surrounding environment (see *Procession*). A path links these experiences together. It does not need to be a real, physical line on the ground but can be implied or imaginary (see *Axis*, *Alignment* and *Containment*) or even partially obscured. When identifying a path, people look for void spaces between solid forms that have linear depth that suggest that we can travel through or between them to get somewhere else. We look for points of contrast, patterns that imply direction and for smoothness or ease of travel. We will often look for the shortest route from where we are to where we wish to go. There may be several events or intermediate goals along a path that enrich the overall experience, mark something important, reinforce its character or its usefulness (see *Journey*). Many paths are appreciated for the opportunities and interest they create rather than just their utility.

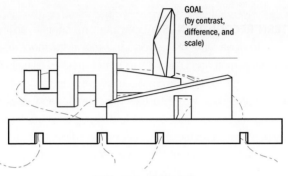

GOAL
(by contrast,
difference, and
scale)

GOAL with (Implied) Path(s)

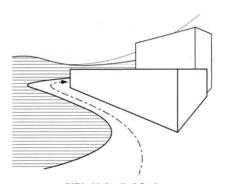

PATH with (Implied) Goal

PATTERN

PATTERN RECOGNITION IS a basic human cognitive ability that allows us to make sense of the world, use known situations to understand unknown situations, and decrease our stress by filling in partial evidences to make complete wholes. It is a basic operation of human thinking that allows us not to have to examine (and re-examine) everything in our environment, over and over. Our natural inclination is to seek patterns and recognize them as an efficient way to understand the world and act in it. Patterns are a type of repetition that organizes a formal arrangement or experience as understandable by creating a configuration which we can recognize (see *Repetition*). Once we understand something to be a pattern, we can easily predict what will happen next, where something might be located or how something might work. Patterns are extremely important in architecture because they are one of the basic operations of making and comprehending human environments. We find patterns at the core of understanding path and circulation, theories of proportion, form-to-activity relationships, recognition of importance, building typology (use-to-form relationships – see *Type*), urban morphology and all ordering principles (see *Axis*, *Centrality* and *Radiosity*).

When we perceive our environment, we look to make sense of it by grouping lots of little things into larger assembles. If we can identify in these assemblies any type of predictable structure caused by regular relationships, known hierarchies and expected proximities, we understand that arrangement as a pattern. Visual patterns are easy to recognize as the information is right before us. When we group elements together through similarity, this is a visual pattern (see *Relationship*). Another common visual pattern is rhythm. Rhythm uses a simple relationship between shapes, attributes, spaces or objects to make a longer more complex sequence through repetition. We might start with something simple like "column-space-window-space" or "black-white-black-black" as a seed to build a more complex field that contains several or even hundreds of repetitions of that sequence. While visual patterns in formal arrangements can be simple or complex depending on the context, they are always something people search out.

The more useful patterns in architecture are not visual but compositional and based on applying past knowledge to new situations. As we inhabit our world, patterns introduce predictability into our built environments – when we encounter an arrangement of shapes or activities that matches something we already know (i.e. they are recurring), we can anticipate what might happen or how we might use the space. As architectural designers, patterns allow us to propose formal spaces we have never known before by using formal and event relationships that we do know. We can do this by identifying and applying compositional arrangements from an existing space to design another space that supports the same or similar human events (see *Pattern Mapping*). The use of a pattern gives us some confidence that we will be creating new spaces and forms that will be successful for the types of activities that might occur there. There are two different types of compositional patterns that are used in architecture and these relate to two different types of information – *formal patterns* and *event patterns*.

Formal patterns are characterized by the regular arrangement of objects in space – those things around us that we can see, touch and move through. Formal patterns are created through aligning solid and voids in meaningful assembles – a "meaningful" assembly is one that is understandable even when partially experienced (i.e. the human brain fills in the pattern even when not directly experienced) or legible because it has occurred before (i.e. the human brain matches the new thing to something already known). If we see the edge of a tile floor that has alternating colour, we can fill in the rest of the floor by continuing the visual pattern in our heads. In a less obvious way, a window is also a pattern. When we see an opening through a wall and there is transparent or translucent material that separates one side from the other, we can easily identify that form as a window. There might be lots of other details that change from one window to another – some might open while others do not, size and aspect might differ wildly between different windows and transparency might be achieved in different ways. However, these details are not part of the pattern of a window as a pattern reduces something to only its key information that defines something for what it is (see *Abstraction*). For a window, the formal pattern is a penetration through a wall that does not support the passage of a human body. In contrast, the pattern of a door is a penetration through a wall that supports a human body. If any aspect of the pattern is absent, then what we have is no longer a window but something else because it no longer matches the formal pattern. Formal patterns are found at all scales of the environment from doorknobs to the arrangement of city sectors.

Event patterns are patterns that describe what the formal composition *does* in its context rather than its physical composition – we cannot always directly see or touch this information, but we can experience it. An event is simply something that happens and for architecture, important contextual events are environmental forces (sun, wind, topography, etc.), social interactions (visibility, movement, etc.) and cultural values (identity, standing, etc.). When we reduce an object to an event pattern, we can ignore its physical nature and, instead, define

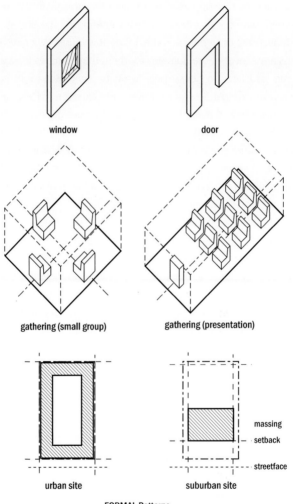

window

door

gathering (small group)

gathering (presentation)

urban site

suburban site

massing
setback
streetface

FORMAL Patterns

the recurring events supported or allowed by that object. In the case of the window, the supported events are allowing light into an interior volume, allowing view into or out of the interior volume, and allowing the movement of air between the adjacent volumes. When we come across any aspect of the built environment that matches this pattern, we can associate this new experience with our known event pattern of a window – regardless to what we might expect it to look like or its traditional physical definition. In architectural design, event patterns allow us to break down objects into their effects and then design to satisfy the same event without being restricted to the same form. For example, the event of a window might be satisfied by three different formal proposals that independently address the transfer of light, the ability to create a view and the passage of fresh air.

The importance of pattern is that it enables us to know something we have not yet experienced. People are very good at completing patterns and it is a human instinct to attempt closure – we make complete objects in our heads out of partial evidences in the world. Patterns are also useful for learning from the world. When a successful environment is reduced to its important patterns (formal and event), we can use that information to design new environments without having to imitate either its style or aesthetics (see *Type*). Another importance aspect of pattern is when a pattern is broken – and for designers, this would be deliberate. We might break a pattern to draw attention to a particular aspect of that environment, to create importance or change hierarchy. As we seek patterns, we also notice things that do not fit, things which are disruptive or potentially dangerous, and things that stand out (see *Difference*). Patterns are one of the ways we make our environment more understandable and more *human*.

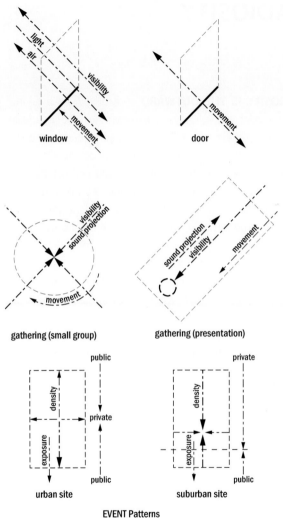

window

door

gathering (small group)

gathering (presentation)

urban site

suburban site

EVENT Patterns

RADIOSITY

RADIOSITY IS THE OUTWARD spreading from a centre. As an ordering principle, radiosity occurs when the real or imaginary centre of a perceived circle (see *Centrality*) is combined with one or more imaginary lines of an axis (see *Axis*). The axis begins at the centre point of the circle, replaces the influence of the perimeter and is understood as either the start or the end point of a path (see *Path-Goal*). Although the perimeter might still be present, the axis becomes dominant through its relationship to the centre. As a comparison, the imaginary lines in an axial system have priority followed by the point they cross while in a centralized system, the centre has priority followed by the perimeter of effect (there are no axial lines). In a radial system, however, the point where the axial lines appear to start or end has priority followed by the axial lines, which appear to terminate or begin at this point. We know that we should move from that point to somewhere else or from somewhere to that point. In either case, the point becomes important. The most common occurrence of a radial ordering system involves multiple axis meeting at a centre so that point is also understood as a type of intersection. A radial intersection differs from an axial intersection due to the centre being dominant over the axis.

The relationship between a centre and an axis in a radial ordering system can also be considered a node as a node is simply a point where lines intersect. The crossing of axes in intersection and grid ordering systems are also nodes. In the same way that an intersection contains a single node while a grid involves the ordered distribution of

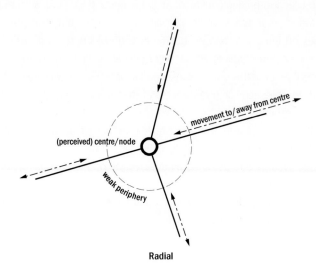

(perceived) centre/node

movement to/ away from centre

weak periphery

Radial

multiple nodes, when we have a single node that stresses centre over axis, we have a radial ordering system. This ordering system is found in multiple contexts from the building to the urban scale. Corridors in a building that move away at different angles from a central space use a radial ordering system. If there were two or more corridors that crossed each other and the corridor space was hierarchically dominant over the point where they crossed, we would have an intersection ordering principle instead. At the larger scale, a radial system is found in urban spaces as an alternative to a grid system. This system relies on important spaces, buildings and objects to work (usually a civic or public space). As all major circulation spaces (corridors or streets) meet at this single point, a radial system sets up a very strong and clear hierarchy of importance that stresses the intersection space over all others.

If we connect several radial systems together, we get a system that uses the nodal ordering principle. While a radial system stresses strong hierarchy with one point dominant over all others, a nodal system can be hierarchical or non-hierarchical. A hierarchical nodal system will have primary, secondary and tertiary levels where some centres and axes are more important than others. In buildings, this might relate to levels of intimacy (public and privateness), connectedness or exposure. In urban spaces, it will mostly be about connectedness, density and social importance. A non-hierarchical nodal system will treat all centres and axes as equal. This latter operates similarly to a grid ordering system except without the requirement to have parallel axial lines or standard spacing pattern.

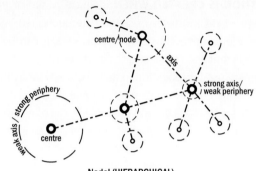

Nodal (HIERARCHICAL)

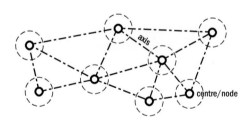

Nodal (NON-HIERARCHICAL)

REPETITION

REPETITION IS CREATED WHEN identical or similar things (i.e. objects, elements, surfaces or spaces) are duplicated in an environment. While repetition seems a basic idea, it can be used for several different and conflicting things depending on the context. The primary use for repetition in architecture is to create a sense of continuous built fabric through sameness. This is one way to create a field effect or a ground in contrast to an object (see *Object-Ground*), create a relationship through similarity (see *Relationship*) or reinforce alignment (see *Alignment*). When the same forms or their attributes are repeated – such as a series of windows on a façade, façades on a street, surface materials or colour palette – those single elements are interpreted as part of a larger whole. Once clustered into a larger group, we no longer consciously address them as individual elements. Repetition suppresses difference by eliminating hierarchy between the elements which then dismisses our direct attention.

In contrast, while repetition makes us pay less attention to some things, it can also make us pay *more* attention to others. Repetition can create a type of reinforcement which indicates that something is important (see *Importance* and *Coherence*). When we see, experience or think about the same thing several times, it is brought more strongly to our awareness as part of our natural ability of identifying patterns in our environment and experiences (see *Pattern*). We perceive the repeated things as a group to which we should pay attention. This works equally for ideas, events and objects. When we encounter the

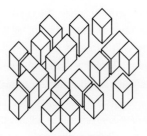

Repetition as FIELD

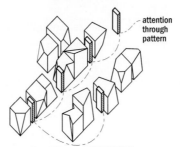

attention
through
pattern

Repetition as IMPORTANCE

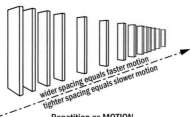

wider spacing equals faster motion
tighter spacing equals slower motion

Repetition as MOTION

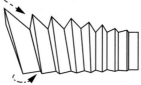

Repetition as TRANSFORMATION

same form (maybe a column), event (perhaps a movement pattern) or compositional element (possibly a long, tall but slim form) several times in our awareness, it suggests that thing *might have* some significance in this context. The effect works the same if it is a word that is said several times (such as your name or "stop"), or an underlying architectural idea occurs more than once (such as an ordering principle like axis or centre). The repetition tells us that we should bring our focus to bear on this aspect of the environment in order to understand something that could affect us. Of course, if the idea or object is repeated too much, it creates ground rather than object and we stop paying attention – the question for designers is to identify this threshold in each context.

The third use for repetition is to imply motion and transformation in static forms. When the same element is repeated in a linear sequence in our perceptual field, we interpret that sequence as one element moving through space (see *Implied Motion*). The sequence does not have to be straight, but each form must be read as successive to the one before – as part of a larger whole. The spacing between the objects is interpreted as how fast or slow the object is moving and the longer we make the sequence, the stronger it will read as a type of implied motion. When a small change is introduced to each successive form, we produce the idea of transformation. These changes suggest we should understand the initial form to be changing its nature by changing its shape (morphology). Both motion and transformation involve repetition that map between space and time. The larger whole that is created through the repeated objects is understood conceptually to be in time rather than space (i.e. the same way we understand sequential panels in a graphic novel).

SIMILARITY

A BASIC ACT OF THINKING for humans is to look for similarity by grouping things together that we perceive to have some association. We do this to make the world around us less complicated and more meaningful. When we find two or more things that are similar through some shared characteristic, we create a link between them. We make categories by grouping or clustering those things linked into a larger conceptual container and, by doing this, reducing the complexity of our world. For humans, deceasing complexity through cutting down the number of things we pay attention to is positive. We also learn by adding new things we experience to existing containers that we have already formed, allowing the previously unknown to be known and meaningful. It does not matter if those things are ideas, events or objects; the thinking process works in the same way. This act of grouping is one of the main operations behind analytical or convergent thinking. Our environment becomes familiar through the identification of similarity and the resulting categorization and organization. There are two ways similarity operates in architecture – through *formal associations* and *spatialized events*.

Formal associations are recognized in our built environment through the *visual interpretation of formal attributes*. This means that we group things together based on what they look like – we seek out similarity in shape, size, material, texture and colour. Similarity can be applied to an ordering principle to reinforce the intended understanding and use of that space (see *Alignment*, *Axis*, *Centrality* and *Radiosity*) as well as spaces that do not have a formal ordering system. Five buildings of the same size or same exterior material will be understood as part of a larger group even if they are not aligned to an axis, edge or centre and even if other attributes are different (such as same size but different colours, material and shape). Several floor areas with the same material can be placed next to other floor areas with a different material. The areas with the same material will be grouped in our heads as one type of space while the second material surface will create a second type of space. Our act of looking for similarity and creating associations through this concept is so strong that we will automatically create separate spaces even if the floor areas are in a single room and not divided by physical objects such as walls.

The second type of similarity is understood through *events* that take place in space (i.e. movement, activities, behaviours). We can understand spaces by grouping based on what happens in them and the similarity of their activities. If we consider a dining room, a cafeteria and a restaurant from a formal point of view, each of these spaces may be different in terms of size, shape, materials and surface textures. However, if we look at activities in each of these locations, we can understand all three spaces as similar as they share the event of eating food.

Similarity has several different effects and uses as part of other thinking skills and design operations. It can create perceived wholes out of parts (see *Alignment*), define containers and different states of spaces (see *Containment*), create known associations (see *Relationship*), define patterns and types (see *Pattern* and *Type*) and allow us to design new spaces by understanding existing ones (see *Pattern Mapping*).

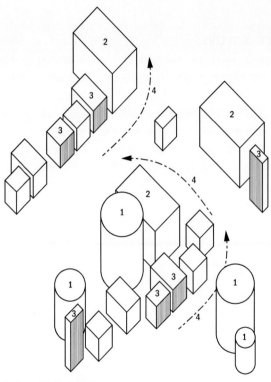

1. shape similarity (cylinder)
2. scale similarity (large orthotope)
3. texture similarity (creation of front)
4. event similarity (movement pattern)

SOLID-VOID

WE LIVE OUR LIVES in the empty space on and between solids. Our physical reality could be said to be defined simply by those two things: the solids with which we interact (see, touch, walk on, move through, climb within, brush against) and the void space between those solids which *allow*s those interactions. Both solid and void are ways to define a volume of space but conceptually we understand solids as a volume which is "full" and void as a volume that is "empty". This is why solid is also known as positive space (something is there) while void is called negative space (something is not there). Each of these two ideas is defined through the other – solids exist because void allows them to be perceptible, distinct and discrete (individually separate). Void is defined in the presence of an adjacent solid and it is only when void is bounded that it comes into our awareness (see *Objectification* and *Containment*). The relationship between solid and void is the basis of formal architectural design.

The solid-void relationship in architecture is engaged through the manipulation and arrangement of surfaces in a four-dimensional environment (depth, width, height and time). When we experience the environments we inhabit, we project outwards with our senses from our centres – our bodies – and come first into contact with the surfaces of the solids around us. Our bodies move through space such that no surface is perceived from a static point of view but involves changing perspectives. As we move, surfaces are understood as part of a spatial sequence that is activated by tracing a path through an environment (see *Procession*). The solid behind the surface, the mass,

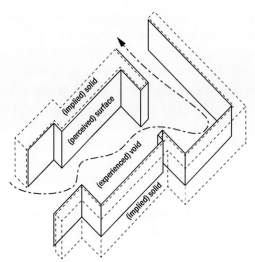

Solid as PERCEIVED SURFACE and Implied Mass

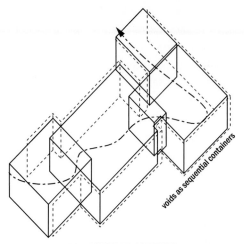

Void as PERCEIVED CONTAINER

is implied but never directly experienced. The empty space in front of the surface, the void, is experienced but not *directly* perceivable. Instead, we construct a three-dimensional boundary from the visible surfaces to conceptually enclose that space. By doing this, we convert intangible space into a tangible object that is familiar to us – a container. It could be said that architecture is the shaping of sequential voids rather than the construction of static solids because it is in the void (the container) that the human dwells.

Once we have made solid and void into distinct, separate objects in our minds, we can manipulate them for design intentions. Hierarchically, we can have one of three major positions; either the solid is dominant, the void is dominant or the solid and void are more equal in importance. An environment where a solid is perceived to have been added to a void, the solid is the active element and the void is perceived as neutral space. The solid tends towards surfaces that express object rather than ground (see *Object-Ground*), distinctness (see *Difference*) and wholeness. This later means that the surface encloses a volume of space so that it expresses mass either as a large whole or a series of smaller elements added together (aggregate forms). Dominant solids are used for points of importance, as focus in axis and goals in journeys. In contrast, when the void is the active element, we see the solid as the neutral element from which space has been carved. It is the empty space that expresses wholeness and convexity instead of the solid. The visible surfaces are understood as belonging to the void – i.e. the inner surface of a perceived container rather than the outer surface of a perceived mass. Dominant voids are used for alignment as well as strong centrality and axial relationships. Built environments can also achieve a balance between solid and void relationships.

Dominant SOLID

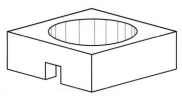

Dominant VOID

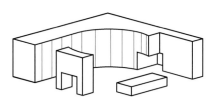

BALANCED Solid and Void

MAKING ARCHITECTURE THROUGH BEING HUMAN

SITUATED NOTIONS

ARCHITECTURE INVOLVES IDEAS that relate forms to other forms in voids as expressed through their surfaces. How we associate these forms with each other and ourselves is not arbitrary as architecture satisfies a human need – it creates environments that are for *us*, with which *we* identify and that satisfy *our* requirements from shelter to self-actualization. This means that architectural forms and their visible surfaces are not self-referential (only about themselves) but are successful based on how well they satisfy events generated by the needs of people. These events can range from the simple (allowing light into an interior) to complex (expressing cultural belief systems). They also must affect the physical environment, be spatially located and exist at a certain scale that is reasonable to be understood and engaged by a human body. Every act of architecture responds to ideas that are located in a *particular context* with *particular characteristics* leading to *particular forms* that respond directly to that context. This is known as spatialized and situated knowledge.

The first section introduced concepts based on how our bodies influence our understanding of the world. This section builds on those ideas and extends basic concepts into situated knowledge. There is not a strict separation between these two sections as formal concepts are also spatially located. However, situated notions use formal concepts by either extending their basic ideas, connecting two or more concepts or grouping several concepts together based on their effect. Situated notions tend towards increased complexity and are more abstract. Their direct effect in the built environment is present but less identifiable.

CONTAINMENT

PEOPLE PUT BOUNDARIES around ideas, experiences and phe- nomena (i.e. void, air, light, temperature) to understand them. We make things that are not physically solid into objects so we can engage, understand or manipulate them (see *Objectification*). When an object has something inside it, we understand that thing as a container. A container is a special type of object because while it has edges and surfaces like all objects, it also includes the ideas of inside, outside, boundary, content and entrance. Our experience with containers means that we know that they can be open or closed and either full or empty, conditions which imply access and content. These are important ideas as containers create a volume of space that is rec- ognizably not the same as what is around it regardless if the container is literal (i.e. there is a physical boundary) or conceptual (we imagine a boundary). When we divide our world and the things in it into cat- egories, groups, sections, classes or ranks – this is an act of contain- ment. When we connect three edges, a change in surface and an alignment to imply one space has different activities to another, this is also an act of containment.

One of the most important ideas about containment is how *inside* and *outside* allow us to make or deny relationships through *associ- ation* and *separation*. If we draw an imaginary line around several things, put objects together in a box, group things together in our heads, or place people together in a room, we understand these things to be *inside* through containment. The boundary of the con- tainer creates an expected association between things inside through

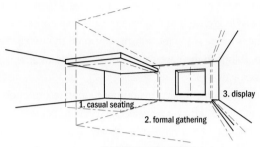

Containers and activities

1. casual seating
2. formal gathering
3. display

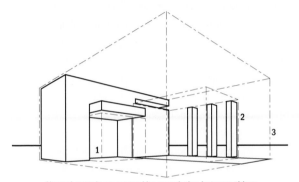

Nested containers created by association between things

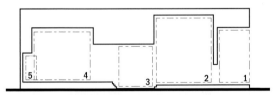

Sequential containers in formal composition

implied sameness and proximity (see *Relationship*). The opposite is also true. Once we understand something to have an inside, it naturally has an *outside* as well. Anything located outside is considered separate to what is inside – any relationship between the two is denied or repressed. Things, in this case, can be ideas, objects, people, events, experiences or activities.

Containment in the built environment operates through any *implied boundary* created by a perceived association between things, a perceived change of environmental quality or a change in formal composition. These might include a change in ceiling form or height; the projection of building mass over an exterior area; the similarity of objects along a perimeter; a transition in quality of light; a change of material in the ground plane; the alignment of architectural objects such as stairs, ramps, platforms or columns to create bounded associations; or a change of grade that produces at least two edges. Containment is produced by the creation of an imaginary (but cognitively real) separation between spaces.

We use containment to organize formal composition to support human events. Much of the content that shapes the size, composition, detail and materiality of buildings and rooms is based on experiences and activities of people that use those spaces. If we consider two events, such as sitting casually talking to a few friends or attending a large, formal dinner, we understand that each activity takes up a particular amount of space of a particular shape and with particular materials. In addition, there are artefacts (objects, fixtures, furnishings) associated with that activity which also have a particular arrangement as well as qualities of the environment supporting that activity (lighting, air temperature, view, topography and so on) and qualities associated with time of occurrence and duration of the event. When there is a difference in how the formal space supports each human event, this is reflected in some aspect of composition, materiality, artefacts, arrangement and spatial quality. That difference creates a separation that can be experienced through how we bound those events. For example, two upholstered chairs in front of a small window with a dropped ceiling might be next to a large table centred under a lighting fixture and positioned on the major room axis supported by a large window and a raised ceiling area in a room. The relationship between the artefacts (chairs, tables, rugs) and the formal composition (dropped or raised ceilings, windows, floor material) will create two *different* contained spaces within another larger physical contained space (the room). When we experience or design a building or room, we use containment to create implied separations, areas of focus, areas of isolation and suggestions of use by implying boundaries, even if there is no physical separation.

Containment operates at multiple scales and we find containers next to other containers inside larger containers moving from the small to the very large (this is part of our ability to create layers through *Hierarchy*). The same notion that allows us to understand a quiet meeting nook as separate to a main dining room also allows us to organize a program by associating related activities into groups or clusters within a site bound through property lines that are not physically real (see *Program*). Zoning is an idea of containment that operates at an urban scale to restrict building use types to particular areas. Superimposition (the placement of two program elements on top of each other) interlacing (the weaving of two program elements where each maintains its identity), and nesting (the layering of one program element within another) are only possible due to our understanding of containment.

DIMENSIONALITY

THE TERM "DIMENSION" HAS become a shorthand for "measurement", but this is an extremely limited way to consider a very important idea. More precisely, a dimension is a *layer of information connected to a property*. A property can be either an attribute (physical descriptions such as length, width, height, texture, weight, temperature, colour, solidity, luminosity, reflectivity), a quality (cultural and sensory descriptions such as smell, age, value, status, timeliness, emotions) or a characteristic (event descriptions such as duration, speed, rotation, momentum). If we consider a piece of paper, for example, the standard way of considering this object is as "two-dimensional". However, the paper also has depth through its thickness (ranging from tissue to cardstock); it has texture (from smooth to rough or patterned); the surface might be gloss or matt; the paper has real weight but it also has perceived weight; it has cultural status (cheap lined notepad or watercolour rag); and so on. Each of these properties is a dimension of information of the paper. The two-dimensional paper has, in this case, *at least* nine important dimensions that should be engaged by a designer – length, width, thickness, texture, colour, reflectivity, real weight, perceived weight and perceived status.

If we restrict our understanding of dimensions in architecture to simply the length, width and depth of objects placed in the environment, we would create an artificially narrow, and fairly shallow, set of design options. As we can see from the paper example, there are many more physical dimensions of knowledge related to something that seems simple and architectural objects are not simple. This is

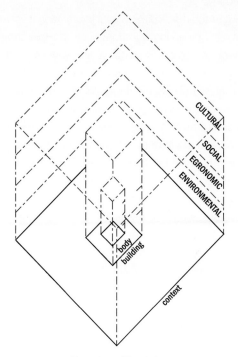

Dimensions of Knowledge

because architecture is responsible to construct *human environments* for *human events*. This means that added to the physical dimensions, there is information that is psychological, social and cultural (i.e. human-to-human) involving qualities and characteristics rather than simply attributes.

We can start to unpack dimensional information involved in architectural projects by asking questions such as: How should a body move through this space? How do we know where to go or where we should go? How do we shape form to support different types of human activities? How should the building engage its surrounding context? How do the architectural forms respond to issues of human happiness or health? What aspects respond to how we see ourselves as individuals, as a group or as a culture? Some of these answers will be practical, others will be metaphysical or considered as an extension of identity or expression. Thinking about these questions, we can understand that architectural design includes dimensions of knowledge that address environmental factors (physical protection), human body ergonomics (physical comfort), social engagement (facilitating human interaction) and cultural identity (expressing who we are).

Environmental factors will range from formal responses to sunlight, ambient temperature, and shadow to the shaping of the ground (topography). Between these, there is wind and water – as rain, flood and humidity. These dimensions include knowledge which is measurable including sun angle, air movement, humidity, precipitation rate, ground slope, thermal capacity, sound transfer and so on.

Ergonomic dimensions will stress how things touch the human body, how we move through space (see *Journey* and *Procession*), and how things are made for us (i.e. humans). Most of these are also measurable and testable. We can try something out and see if our hand uses a railing better if shaped *this* way with *that* material. We can suggest and then examine if a path of travel through a building is easy to understand or if the arrangement of elements in a room make it easier or harder to use that room.

Social dimensions involve how objects and space interact to affect people engaging other people. These are about activities and include issues of publicness and privacy, gathering (see *Convexity*), exposure or isolation through physical connections (see *Connectedness*), sound and sightlines (see *Exposure*), various types of movement from stillness to high activity (see *Journey*) and issues of perceived and actual security.

Cultural dimensions are about identity – they address how we see ourselves or how we wish others to see us, what values we hold, and what we think matters (see *Identity* and *Presence*). This ranges from an individual, to a family, organization, neighbourhood, city and nation. Dimensional information in the cultural category address historical positions, cultural norms and media representations. Most of this knowledge is in the realm of beliefs and is not factual or test-able. However, it can be described, debated and identified through human-to-human agreement and will be relevant to architecture if it produces an effect or change in the formal environment.

We can understand how the identification of dimensional know-ledge is an important skill to learn as an architectural designer if we take something that seems basic such as a door. A door can be said to be a simple, physical artefact. Its primary dimensions are width and height. The event it supports is the movement through a solid plane. However, we can quickly start to unpack additional dimensions of knowledge attached to the door's size and materiality. First, the size of a door contains more information than simply height and width. It can tell us social information such as if the door is private (small, narrow, discrete) or public (large, expressive, monumental), meant for one person (single door) or several (double door). The materiality of the door contains dimensional information that includes environmental (resist thermal transfer and drafts), ergonomic (how do we open it), social (allows exposure or creates privacy and security) and cultural (what does the door say about us?). We can continue to expand the dimensionality of the door through some more questions such as: How should the hand reach to open the door? What should be the perceived weight of the door, should it look heavy or light? What about actual weight? How should the door express entrance? How should it engage the street? Where should it be visible from and how does it interact with path and circulation? Responding to these questions through design decisions creates multi-dimensional content. When a project, object or situation has dimensionality, we consider it to have *depth* (i.e. dimensional depth) through the clear consideration of multiple properties in a layered response.

Dimensional knowledge in architecture is found at several different scales ranging from the hand on a railing to the presence of a building form in a city's identity. One of the difficulties of architectural design is the organization and construction of relationships between information that occur at least three major scales *at the same time* – the body, the building and its context (see *Coherence* and *Cohesiveness*). In addition, not all dimensions of knowledge will be as relevant for all contexts. It is necessary to be able to recognize which dimension of knowledge matters most for the particular design situation (see *Hierarchy*).

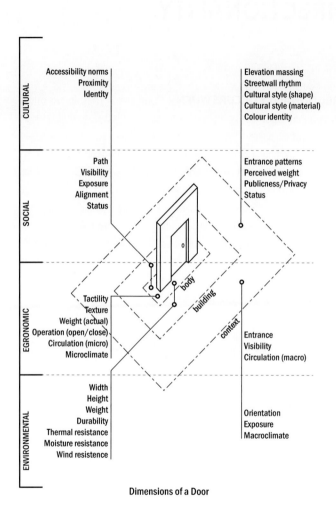

CULTURAL

Accessibility norms
Proximity
Identity

Elevation massing
Streetwall rhythm
Cultural style (shape)
Cultural style (material)
Colour identity

SOCIAL

Path
Visibility
Exposure
Alignment
Status

Entrance patterns
Perceived weight
Publicness/Privacy
Status

EGRONOMIC

Tactility
Texture
Weight (actual)
Operation (open/close)
Circulation (micro)
Microclimate

Entrance
Visibility
Circulation (macro)

ENVIRONMENTAL

Width
Height
Weight
Durability
Thermal resistance
Moisture resistance
Wind resistence

Orientation
Exposure
Macroclimate

body
building
context

Dimensions of a Door

DIRECTIONALITY

DIRECTIONALITY OCCURS WHEN we perceive something as prioritizing one direction over others within a space. It is the inevitable result of objects and spaces that are understood to have an orientation (see *Orientation*). While orientation is about the object itself, directionality is about how the object might engage its environment. Directionality is created when objects and spaces imply the ability to project into the environment either through extended gaze (see *Proximity*), an imaginary axis (see *Axis*) or the suggestion of movement in one direction (see *Implied Motion*). We orientate and extend objects without thinking as it is part of how we understand ourselves – the ability to look, speak, reach, hold and move are all directional actions. As we understand the environment through ourselves and our interaction with other humans, no object in the environment can be understood simply as an inert shape. In the case of directionality, we look for a primary plane, primary axis or gesture of forward motion (projected path) using formal hierarchy.

A primary plane is created when we identify one side of an object or space as hierarchically more important than other surfaces (see *Front*). This plane becomes understood as the point of engagement between that object or space and its surrounding environment through projecting its presence or implied gaze outwards. Once a front is determined, any interaction or relationship will be expected to originate forward from that plane.

A primary axis is created when one axis creates difference through formal properties (i.e. scale, height, width, texture, materiality) from

**No Axis,
NO DIRECTIONALITY**

**One Axis,
NO DIRECTIONALITY**

**Two Equal Axes,
NO DIRECTIONALITY**

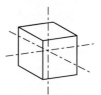

**Three Equal Axes,
NO DIRECTIONALITY**

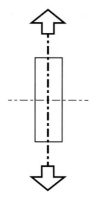

**Two Non-equal Axes,
Producing DIRECTIONALITY**

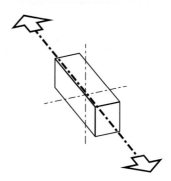

**Three Non-equal Axes,
Producing DIRECTIONALITY**

the others. That axis will be perceived as an imaginary line that extends away from the object, giving it a sense of directionality. One of the easiest ways to form a primary axis is through the creation of sides with unequal lengths. When two parallel sides of an object are longer than the width or height, and there are no other modifying factors such as the introduction of front, the longer sides create an axis that is considered more significant or primary.

A projected path occurs when we interpret a form that not only has a primary axis but is able to "move" along that axis (see *Implied Motion*). We understand paths from our experience with moving objects and we give the same notion to non-moving objects. The path is created through interpreting forward motion of an object through its formal composition. Sloped, smooth, thin and repeated objects extending along a primary axis will imply forward motion. Forward motion will then inscribe a projected path which the object *would* follow if it *could* move.

As an example of directionality, we can consider a simple object in the built environment such as a column. A column that is square and has no difference in detail or materiality on any side does not have directionality. However, if that square column had one side that was textured, coloured differently or involved some other element of difference, that side would be interpreted as a front and has directionality through projected gaze. A column that is rectangular rather than square would have directionality through a primary axis. If the column was tapered to a point on side and even curved slightly, we would understand the column as projecting along a path extending from the direction of implied motion. All these things only occur in our minds but this does not mean they are not real, only that they are not factual.

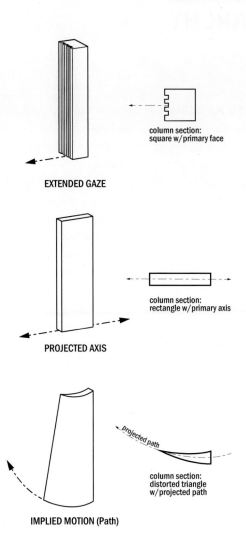

EXTENDED GAZE

column section:
square w/ primary face

PROJECTED AXIS

column section:
rectangle w/ primary axis

projected path

column section:
distorted triangle
w/ projected path

IMPLIED MOTION (Path)

HIERARCHY

HIERARCHY IS A SYSTEM of organization that arranges things based on categories of belonging or relative importance. It is used in architectural design in two different ways with two different effects. These are *classification hierarchy* and *formal hierarchy*.

Classification hierarchy allows us to consider how information is organized. As a thinking skill in a design process, classification hierarchy has less to do with authority and more with specificity. We use this hierarchy as a tool to understand the relationship between things based on moving from distinct and precise characteristics to larger and more general categories. If we consider a *cottage* through classification hierarchy, we can easily describe it as belonging to the category of *house* and that a house is a type of *residential building* (three hierarchical levels). We could generalize even further to classify a residential building as a type of *building*, which belongs to the category of a *built structure*, which is a type of *industrial product* and so on. The ability to generalize to a larger category allows us to access all of the information found in that category. Since the knowledge is more general, we might consider it more basic, however the important aspect is that shifting hierarchical levels reveals *different types* of information, relationships and priorities. At the level of *cottage*, we focus on information specific to that idea – scale, materiality and location in context (siting). As we move to the level of *house*, it brings in information about the use and needs of domesticity, while the *residential building* level engages issues of zoning, codes and infrastructure. The more general *building* category is connected to construction and assembly

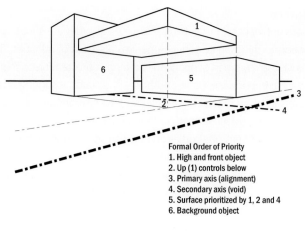

Formal Order of Priority
1. High and front object
2. Up (1) controls below
3. Primary axis (alignment)
4. Secondary axis (void)
5. Surface prioritized by 1, 2 and 4
6. Background object

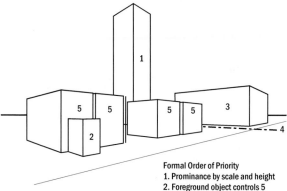

Formal Order of Priority
1. Prominance by scale and height
2. Foreground object controls 5
3. Prominance by scale and alignment
4. Axis created by 1 and 3
5. Similarity creates ground(least concern)

practices. The process of classifying based on hierarchical levels uses object and event abstractions that scale between categories (see *Abstraction*).

Formal hierarchy, in contrast, tells us what order we should pay attention to things in our environment as a system of priorities. This type of hierarchy is part of our need to arrange our attention on things of interest, importance, power, authority and status. It suggests possible relationships between ourselves and the environment as well as allows us to interpret relationships between objects and spaces based on knowledge from our bodies and human social structures. Formal hierarchy is fundamentally a system of judgement.

We use formal hierarchy to create a system of relative importance based on the location, composition and attributes of objects. The knowledge for these interpretations starts with embodied concepts formed by our physical experience and then mapped to our social interactions. The embodied concepts that are relevant to formal hierarchy are proximity, relative position (front or above), scale, height, width, inertia and difference. For humans, the properties and spatial position of something has significant meaning and things that are high, close and big are more important to us than things that are low, distant and small (i.e. they can affect us and, therefore, are important). In general, we will interpret an object above another object as controlling or having more status than what is below. As a function of proximity, objects in front of others (i.e. in our visual foreground) are considered a higher priority than things behind or further away as we understand them as more immediately relevant (see *Object-Ground*). Larger or taller objects draw our attention away from smaller or shorter objects and wider circulation paths have priority over narrower ones. Objects that appear to move will capture our attention before things that are clearly static (see *Implied Motion*) and moments of difference will be seen before things that are the same (see *Difference*). We use this basic knowledge of relative spatial relationships to understand social positioning. Consider for a moment why we describe someone who has authority as "being on top" or "above us" and someone with first rights to something is "in front of" someone else.

While our physical environment is a significant source of how we structure our thinking, what is really interesting is that this influence is not one-directional. We use our knowledge of the environment to understand more abstract things like human social interactions, but we also project our social condition back into the environment to understand it in a much richer way. This means all the knowledge we use to interpret the relationship between people is also used to interpret our relationship with the physical context (see *Relationship*, *Importance*, *Identity* and *Personification*).

Hierarchical concepts can be combined when we design environments and, in application, we hardly ever find them in isolation. Ordering systems that are not equally distributed, such as a grid or nodal system that have different levels of importance between the various centres, intersections or axes will use scale, height, width and difference to organize our attention. Circulation routes that have different hierarchical levels (a main public corridor, a secondary route and private paths, for example) will use width, difference and scale, at a minimum. We need to remember that formal hierarchy is a conceptual ordering system that arranges our attention when we engage complex environments. The goal is to create a contextual *system of priorities* so we can more easily make sense of our environment. The concepts are scaleless until applied to a context, so we find the same ideas present from the scale of the handheld object to the scale of urban compositions.

IDENTITY

IDENTITY IS WHO WE THINK WE ARE and how we understand ourselves as distinct from everything and everyone around us. Our identity is formed by aspects of our belief systems, important values, traits and expressions that are considered significant, foundational or fundamental. While these things are all inside our heads, we express them outwardly through critical actions such as how we choose to live our lives, the choices we make and how we present ourselves to others through body stance, fashion, ornament and the things we arrange around us. The outward expression of identity creates characteristics that are recognizable by others – a primary type of information used to guide interactions and responses. This information allows us to have a sense of those entities with which we interact by projecting aspects of our own identity on to other entities (i.e. we know others through ourselves). Identity in the built environment works in the same way. When considering an architectural form or space, we look for essential characteristics to help us understand "who it is", how to "know" it and, thus, how to interact with it. It is through an interpretation of formal composition and physical attributes that we look to understand the basic quality or purpose of something. This can occur through projecting *character* into forms and spaces or by determining what is the *fundamental purpose* of that thing.

Character works through aligning aspects of an environment towards a known human trait, bearing or expression of conduct as expressed in formal composition through an interpretation of shape and surface qualities (see *Personification* and *Cohesiveness*). Human

Graceful? Elegance? Sleek?

Whimsical? Playful?

Serious? Formal? Uptight?

Identity through CHARACTER

traits might include notions of grace, solidity, dignity, solemnity, pensiveness, frivolity, reservation, whimsicalness or joyfulness. Any human character trait can be transferred to architectural form *if* there are identifiable physical indicators of that character – usually body posture and surface information such as body markings, clothing details (cut, colour, social association) and accessories (see *Metaphor*). The transfer uses our own knowledge of formal elements from social interactions with other humans to create an understanding between ourselves and aspects of the built environment.

When we consider something (most likely a building) to have an architectural style, this is also an expression of character. A style does not generally engage human traits to express identity but instead uses the association of formal characteristics that distinguishes something as unique through the organization of parts and the selection of materials. The relationship between shapes, materials and their assembly then produces a cohesive whole that is *different* from other examples of the same category (i.e. one building is recognisably unlike another). We identify a style because it is distinctive and creates a unique expression of that building or space. We also identify a style because it is repeated – the distinctiveness is shared through similarity which makes style a pattern that uses essential characteristics to produce a general identity rather than a particular personality (see *Type*).

Identity can also be found in objects or spaces through considering their fundamental purpose which will ultimately be expressed in their formal arrangement and physical attributes. Ask yourself what makes a living room a living room rather than a sitting room, family room, den or lounge? Or why is an urban square an urban square and when it is a plaza, courtyard, forecourt or park? Each of these terms for a living room or an urban square mean *almost* the same thing but they also identify important differences (which is why we have different words). To understand the identity of these bounded spaces, we can reduce each to its fundamental purpose or identify the unique qualities of the form and space which makes it distinct (see *Spatial Quality*).

Identity through fundamental purpose can be understood through spatial qualities organized by formal or event patterns (see *Pattern*). If we consider something such as a bedroom, its identity can be understood in these two different ways by asking the same question – what makes a bedroom a bedroom? Addressing this question through formal information, we can reduce the bedroom to a range of length-to-width ratios, range of expected area, successful surface materiality, standard circulation pattern and pattern of window size and placement. The relationship between these formal elements gives us the fundamental qualities that allows us to recognize a bedroom when we see one and makes that space significantly different to other types of spaces. If we address the same question but consider event information, we can describe the identity of a bedroom by what the formal arrangement allows us *to do* rather than how it looks. Identity through events would consider the nature of the relationship between the degree of privacy, quality of light, sound isolation and the connectivity to other spaces. Form and event both allow us to recognize a bedroom as having the identity of a place to sleep but they use different types of information to arrive at a fundamental pattern. They are also used for different purposes – the identification and reproduction of formal identity allows for us to find similarity and familiarity in our environments while event identity allows us to abandon expected forms but still successfully design for what something does (purpose) rather than how it looks.

IMPLIED ACTION

WE LIVE IN A WORLD that is dynamic – things around us act, react, move, change and respond differently from one moment to the next. We expect animate objects and phenomena such as people, animals and weather to make actions and influence their surroundings. However, we also look for the same type of information when we engage static objects such as things in our built environment, including spaces that we make into objects (see *Objectification*). When we interpret one space as penetrating another space, this is an action that does not exist and is performed by something that is not really an object. This action occurs only in our minds and is generated by our preferred way of seeing the world. We use clues found in the formal composition of the environment to give something an action that is not real.

Implied action occurs when any formal characteristic of a static object or space suggests an action that does not actually happen. The form is interpreted as existing in a frozen moment between what might have happened and what might still happen. It is part of the same process of how we give motion to things that are not in motion (see *Implied Motion*) or instability to things that are stable (see *Implied Stability*). In fact, motion can be considered as a type of action that includes a change in location. There are three ways that we understand implied action as suggested through formal information. These are basic actions using dynamic forces, actions using general agency and actions using human agency.

One of the fundamental ways that we give things actions is through interpreting static forms through dynamic forces. These are

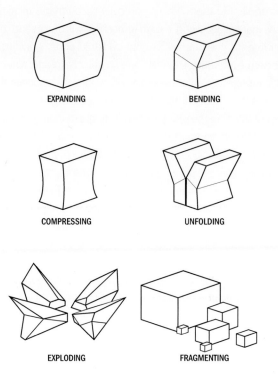

EXPANDING

BENDING

COMPRESSING

UNFOLDING

EXPLODING

FRAGMENTING

Action through DYNAMIC FORCES

events that we know from our environment caused by gravitational, fluid (air and water pressure or movement), exothermic (heat), endothermic (cold) and tectonic forces. Forms that actively have these forces applied to them have a particular shape that is related to the actions that are occurring. A form under heat will distort and melt, one under intense pressure will crumple, a liquid under gravity will flow and extreme internal forces will make an object explode. When we see a static representation of these known events, we associate the form with the action. As such, objects whose shape is aligned with what we expect of things in the process of exploding, expanding, compressing, freezing, folding, bending, flowing or fragmenting will be understood as if that action was occurring even when it is not present.

Implied action also occurs through giving objects a general agency. When something is perceived to happen in the environment, we understand that something else caused it to happen (an agent). Agency is involved in all instances of caused motion as well as how we perceive objects interact with other objects and phenomena. Implied action is present when objects seem to penetrate, push, entangle, squish, tear, twist, slice or pull other parts of the environment. It also occurs when we perceive a form opening towards light, with the phenomenon of light as the agent. Again, we treat the static form as if it were only a moment in a longer series of events.

When something is given the ability to act that is particularly human, these are instances of human agency (see *Personification*). In these cases, we might imagine forms using hands, arms, bodies or feet which are not literal but still change the way we understand the object. It is through implied action that we overlay narratives onto static formal relationships as a way to enrich our interpretation of our environment.

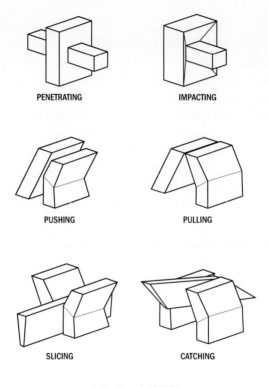

PENETRATING

IMPACTING

PUSHING

PULLING

SLICING

CATCHING

Action through AGENCY

IMPLIED MOTION

MOTION IS IMPORTANT INFORMATION in our environment. People learn at an early age to tell the difference between things that *can* move, things that *should* move and things that *might* move. We know if something can move on its own even if it is not alive as it tends to follow a predictable trajectory (self-motion). We know if something is alive and can move on its own as it shows the ability to vary its motion without the application of an external force (animate motion). And we understand a thing without its own ability to move might still be given motion through an interaction with something else that makes it move (caused motion). Motion is such an important part of our lives that we also make things that literally cannot move seem as if they are moving. This is called implied motion, the projection of a sense of motion into objects that are not in motion.

When people interpret things in the environment which are not factual (they exist in our minds, not in the world), these are created by our ability to project a tendency of an object into a future state of *what might happen* (see *Extrapolation*). That future state becomes one type of information that we use to give meaning to the environment even though that implied event does not happen. For implied motion, the future state is a change in physical location and created through interpreting static objects in our environment based on their physical properties (shape, materiality) or their repetition (see *Repetition*). The object might be a real, physical element, such as a building, wall or stair or it might be something we make into an object such as bounded space (see *Solid-Void*). We decide that these objects

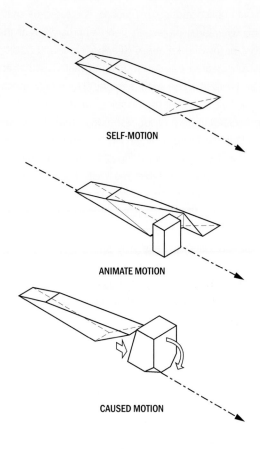

SELF-MOTION

ANIMATE MOTION

CAUSED MOTION

have momentum, speed and trajectories based on visual information of form. It is our experience with things that do move that allows us to give the same abilities to things that do not move.

The basic implied motion, *self-motion*, is created by shapes that are strongly directional, projecting along a primary axis aligned with a clear front or forward tendency (see *Axis*, *Front* and *Directionality*). This is usually created through forms and materials that are aerodynamic and responsive to wind pressure, objects with much longer lengths than heights or widths, or objects that are repeated several times (or several hundred) to suggest momentum along a trajectory (see *Repetition*). The key is directionality as a streamlined object that is not directional, such as a dome, does not imply motion but rather appears to be simply very stable (see *Implied Stability*). When directionality is present, aerodynamic shapes or spaces, smooth materials, thin elements or continuous forms aligning with the major direction will increase the perception of speed. Long spaces with a strong primary axis are more likely to be seen as having forward motion. Spaces that have smooth surfaces and few obstacles (such as being without places where people stop and interact) are interpreted as faster than spaces with more textured surfaces or are compartmentalized. Self-motion occurs when a form is interpreted as having implied motion but does not react to other elements in its surrounding environment.

When an object has implied motion but can be interpreted as reacting to its surroundings, this is understood as *animate motion*. In these situations, we give the objects the abilities of an living organism interpreted through its perceived behaviour as suggested by its form. A linear object that extends into a space is considered to be "travelling" through that area, using a notion of time to explain an idea of space. If there was an obstacle in the path of the object, and the object stopped at that obstacle, we would still understand the situation as an inanimate self-motion. However, if the linear object moved around the obstacle with a series of changes in direction, we now consider the object to be animate since it is obviously reacting to stimuli from its surroundings. We also find animate motion when we interpret forms as having a particular mode of motion – something that is running, twisting, slipping, dodging, jumping, staggering or stumbling as understood through its formal characteristics.

Another type of implied motion, *caused motion*, is created through the interpretation of one form acting on another where the result of that action is implied motion in the second form. We understand a person pushing something will result in the motion of that second thing and interpret the relationship between forms in the same way. To have caused motion, there must be at least two elements present. There also must be some part of the built environment that can be interpreted as expressing a dynamic force (see *Implied Action*). That force must then interact with a second part of the environment which has directionality away from the source of the perceived force. We create a relationship between the two parts of the environment and understand that the first has caused the second to occur. The result is usually inanimate motion from the common causes of being pushed, hit, shoved, knocked or another sort of external, physical pressure. That pressure is only implied, however, and does not really exist.

IMPLIED STABILITY

IMPLIED STABILITY OCCURS when we interpret things in our environment as being extremely balanced, being unstable and close to collapsing or somewhere between these two states. The implication of stability is a separate property to whether that thing is physically stable – that is, we can make something look precarious while it is physically and structurally firm. Rather than a physical fact, implied stability is a conceptual property that we project into our environment as an extension of our natural sense of balance developed through the experience of our body interacting with gravity, weight and momentum (see *Balance*). We know that standing on two legs with a low centre gravity means we are very stable while leaning sideward on one leg and reaching for something is an inherently unstable position for our bodies. We know that things that are thin and tall should be less stable than things that are short and wide. However, strength is not simply a property of visual appearance and we often have a difference between the facts and the perception of stability.

Implied stability is a type of caused motion where gravity and lateral forces (sideward forces such as wind, water or earth pressure) are interpreted to act on perceived mass, weight or density of an object (see *Implied Motion*). Since we feel gravity pushing all things to the surface of the earth, we expect all objects to be on the ground based on this downwards pressure. We know that larger and heavier objects exert a larger downward force and these objects also have greater momentum. Stability is created when downward forces are balanced with upward forces and side-to-side forces cancel each other out.

Both boxes are the same size and
structurally sound but a change in
column dimension changes
perception of weight and stability

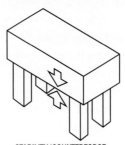

STABILITY/COUNTERFORCE

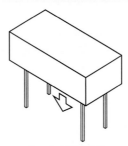

(Perceived) PRESSURE

While this is a physical fact of our environment, we use the same information to interpret visual information. Objects that *appear* to be very heavy or dense will need the perception of a larger upwards force to make them feel stable. Light and diaphanous forms that seem to be tied to the ground will be perceived as straining to lift into the air. While we design for real forces through statics, we also design for perceived forces through formal characteristics.

Implied stability creates events that do not really exist but are present through human interpretation as tendencies that *might happen* (but will not). If an object (building, column, façade) is leaning, then we understand that it would have the *tendency* to continue to lean until it fell. If there is something that appears heavily suspended off the ground, we understand it has a *tendency* to push downward and creates the perception of pressure underneath it. Any object might be stable but can be interpreted as being unstable simply by its shape and other formal characteristics that engage our innate knowledge of gravity. If we were to continue the tendency of downwards momentum to its expected conclusion, we interpret that those objects might collapse, bend, twist, slip, rotate, squeeze or be squeezed. Our interpretation of stability also allows for buildings and building elements to stand firm, to push against each other, to create moments of pressure, to feel heavy, to float with lightness, to stretch, lean and soar (while they do none of those things). Balance is a worthy goal in many architectural projects as it relates to people's natural sense of "rightness". However, there are times when an architectural designer might wish to create a sense of imbalance or instability as an act of attention, focus or drama.

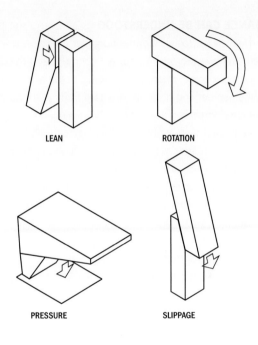

LEAN

ROTATION

PRESSURE

SLIPPAGE

GRAVITATIONAL and LATERAL FORCES

IMPORTANCE

IMPORTANCE CAN BE UNDERSTOOD as an event, substance or object on which we focus our attention. Our attention is a type of judgement that we project into our environment and through that judgement, we decide what value a thing holds and what might matter. When something distinguishes itself from its surroundings or draws our attention, this is an act of the human mind (see *Difference*). Importance is a contextual notion and operates through the relative relationships in a situation. A thing that might have importance in one context could be unimportant in another.

In our built environment, we constantly use the idea of importance to make sense of our surroundings as well as a design tool. It is one of the ways we make what might be a random environment into something comprehensible through the introduction of hierarchy, ordering systems such as axis and centrality, types of repetition, manipulation of light and object attributes that create difference.

The most obvious form of importance is the introduction of difference through the spatial location concepts of *close* and *high* as well as the scalar attribute of *big*. These concepts create a simple hierarchy based on relative relationships. Generally, if an object is close or appears to be close, people will consider it more important than something further away. An object or space located relatively high in an environment is considered more important than things that appear lower or below it. People generally consider something that is big as more important than something that is small (small things are often discounted as irrelevant or not mattering – which causes

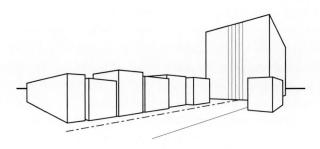

Importance using AXIS, SCALE, DETAIL, HEIGHT

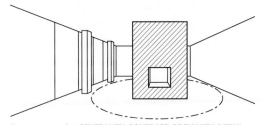

Importance using CENTRALITY, CONTRAST, PROXIMITY, DETAIL

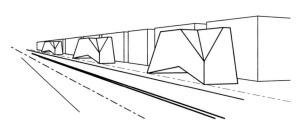

Importance using REPETITION, DIFFERENCE, AXIS, ALIGNMENT, FRONT

its own problems). Big and high have other meanings in human thinking, primarily connected to social status. Buildings that are considered socially or culturally important or to contain important events are often made to be prominent through being big. Height is associated with social status and power – the executive boardroom of a successful corporation is found high in buildings not only for the view but because it expresses power and control.

Ordering systems using axis and centrality introduce a spatial hierarchy that can create importance. An axis is not just an imaginary line in the environment, but a line that can bring attention to an object that interrupts its path (see *Axis*). The form and directionality of the axis creates a focus as it terminates at an object – perhaps a door, window, statue, fountain or building façade (the last is known as a terminated vista). In our heads, we understand the axis as "pointing" at the object, isolating it from the background through drawing our attention. The relationship between the axis and the presence of an object at its perceived termination creates a focus and makes that thing important. In contrast to the linearity of axis, centrality creates importance through a natural human interpretation that centres have a higher priority for attention than peripheral spaces (see *Centrality*). This means that an object or form that is understood as being in a central position is considered more important than something that is found on the outer edges. Formally, it might be a point through which multiple axes converge (denying directionality but making centre), a void or object within a strong boundary form or a radial or convex space with an implied or real boundary. Centrality is always defined by a boundary (real or implied) as a centre does not exist without an edge.

Repetition can also create importance in some situations – but not all. When repetition creates an identifiable pattern that can isolate an element or a set of relationship from a background, we pay attention to that pattern and give it importance (see *Pattern*). For example, if we look across a space filled with objects and planes of all different sizes, colours and materials, there is little that might jump out at first. However, if we notice an object or attribute in this scene repeated several times (maybe a texture, colour, particular shape or element), the pattern that is created makes those things stand out against the perceived randomness of the background.

The introduction and control of light in a context can be used to draw attention and, thus, create moments of importance. The major tools are contrast, brightness and luminosity through the interaction of light with surface materials and qualities such as colour, texture and lustre. An object that is significantly brighter than its surroundings will attract attention through contrast, while areas of relative greater brightness will be important due to how it attracts human attention and encourages movement (humans are phototaxic – we move towards light). The introduction of a skylight into an enclosed space will make an area of that room more important or significant than surrounding, darker areas. When luminosity or shininess is present, our eyes are naturally attracted to that location and we give importance to that area or environmental object.

Importance is used to introduce hierarchy and priority into the built environment to allow people to understand how to engage those spaces or to support activities and movement. Many objects that have been assigned importance become used as destinations or goals as part of program design, circulation and architectural pathing (see *Path-Goal*).

JOURNEY

A JOURNEY IS THE ACT OF TRAVELLING from one place to another. The important aspect of a journey is not simply movement, but how that movement links a series of events into a purposeful sequence. For people, a journey is an important notion and we use it to define more than just physical travels through space. We often map ideas of space to describe ideas of time so journey is applied to many life events. Our major journey is the one between our birth and our death but we also describe personal development as a journey in which we are moving forward towards goals. We talk about love and relationships as journeys on which we might use physical events such as falling, containment, blockage and attachment to describe emotional events. In fact, any sequence of events that has purpose, a sense of direction (see *Directionality*) and can be bounded as a linear form (see *Containment*) can be understood as a journey. Journey is one of the basic conceptualizations we use to understand sequences in our life and environment.

We use journey in architecture to consider the design of circulation – how people move through linked spaces in our built environment through associating *events* and *decisions* to formal composition. The importance of the notion is the focus it brings to the quality of experience involved in movement rather than the movement itself. Journeys are an expanded form of path and destination (see *Path-Goal*) that allows us to think about how several spaces might be aligned to a shared goal or how multiple paths might overlay each other but still maintain their individual identities. A journey will include primary and

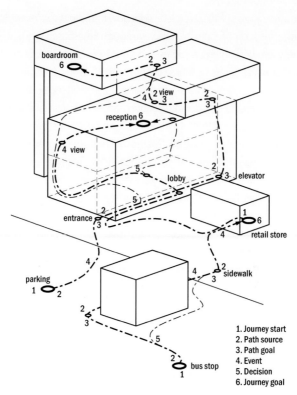

boardroom
6

2 3

4 2 view
    3

2
3

reception 6

4 view

5

lobby

2
3 elevator

5

entrance 2
          3

1
6

retail store

4

4

2 sidewalk
3

parking
1   2

4

2
3

5

1. Journey start
2. Path source
3. Path goal
4. Event
5. Decision
6. Journey goal

2 bus stop
1

PATH, GOAL, EVENT and DECISIONS as Journey

secondary paths, intersections were choices are to be made, major events and opportunities suggested through spatial adjacency or visual connection and goals that might change based on the needs of different occupants.

Journey allows us to start to consider how forms and spaces are linked together into comprehensible wholes through time-based sequences by giving them beginnings, middles and ends (see *Procession*). Beginnings are the starting points or source of movement – front doors, entrances, public transit stops, edges of parking lots, residences, bedrooms, thresholds, street or corridor intersections, and so on. Moments between outside and inside or control points between public and private spaces are natural starting points (see *Threshold*). Ends are our destinations or goals and while these might change for individuals, the arrangement of spaces in buildings usually have a hierarchy with some spaces more likely to be destinations than others. Journey considers the experiences between possible starting points and possible ending points, introducing supportive events or adjacencies to enrich the path and create logical waypoints allowing navigation to be easier. We know that events connected to path can make the journey more interesting and, for people, interesting usually means more meaningful.

The notion of journey operates at multiple scales for architectural designers. The experience of an individual as their body moves through space focuses on information from the human viewshed. Visible information becomes important at this scale as people will scan their surroundings in order to orientate themselves by connecting what they see and creating a mental map to the place they desire to go. As journey includes several spatial sequences, foreshadowing future locations might be included through sightlines, associating spaces through the continuity of material or formally reinforcing ordering principles that connect multiple spaces such as axis, radiosity or node. At the scale of the building, journey is used to organize the relationships between contained spaces, their adjacencies and the events that take place in them (i.e. program elements). These are considered in plan, section and axonometric to make sequences by ordering activities based on exposure, affinity, accessibility, adjacency and publicness/privacy (see *Socio-Spatial Ideas*). At the urban scale, journey is the basis of the movement of human density using activities and zoning (residential to commercial, retail, entertainment) to create relationships between parts of the city through circulation and gathering infrastructure (roads, paths, trails, squares and parks).

While journey is a natural way that people create larger sequences of spaces, events and decisions connected to desires and goals, one issue is that it can introduce a sense of fixed linearity into an environment that is inherently non-linear. The built environment does not have the capacity to convey its content through a rigid delivery system (unlike literature and film). People are free to wander, backtrack or use a different path should they wish. There is no singular focus when we move through our environment – spaces can only suggest the direction of the gaze but not force anyone to look anywhere in a strict order. Different people will experience different things while moving through the same spaces. This means that journey suggests tendencies in directional movement and sequential space – it introduces the *possibility* of movement as a pattern. The inability to directly control our environment as an explicit discourse has benefits – multiple journeys can (and will) coexist within the same space without conflict or confusion if those journeys are constructed to maintain individual identities through minimal levels of hierarchy and coherence. It also means our human spaces are experientially rich environments.

PERSONIFICATION

WHY DO WE SEE FACES in particular arrangements of windows, doors and lintels? Or imagine that a building can reach across a landscape to *touch* or *grasp* some other element without arms and hands? How can we describe a building as happy, sombre, festive, aggressive, sullen or whimsical? Why can two adjacent buildings be understood as leaning against each other or cuddling? None of these descriptions are out of the ordinary but what they describe also does not exist – they are interpretations that have no factual existence outside of our own thoughts. The list above are all examples of *personification* – one of the fundamental ways that we understand objects, spaces, phenomenon and non-human entities by making aspects of them into what we know best: *ourselves*. We simply make what we are considering into a person and then decide what that "person" wants, does or feels. Human characteristics, human emotions, human capacities, human actions, human values and human social interactions are the basis of many of our judgements in the world. In the same way that we make ideas and spaces into objects (see *Objectification*), we make objects into people.

There are four major types of personification that need to be considered by architectural designers. These are *anthropomorphism*, *human agency*, *human social relations* and *human emotional states*. Each is understood through interpreting visual clues of physical form including the shape, apparent mass, texture, colour, materiality and the spatial relationship between objects in the environment.

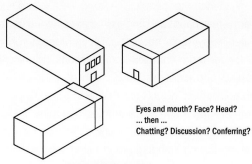

Eyes and mouth? Face? Head?
... then ...
Chatting? Discussion? Conferring?

ANTHROPOMORPHISM

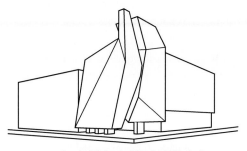

Dancing? Embracing? Nuzzling? Affection?

Human AGENCY

Anthropomorphism occurs when we find aspects of the human body in shapes that are not human. We often attribute faces to patterns found in our built environment as faces are important as sites of engagement for people (see *Front*). We also find references to bodies, arms, feet, hands and fingers in shapes around us. These forms are not literal or symbolic but gestural as anthropomorphism is a tool used to trigger more complex interpretations including emotional states, agency and social relationships. Once we identify an aspect of a human body in a thing, it is not that far of a step to give that thing other human abilities and characteristics. That thing – which include buildings, building elements and spaces – can then be understood to be crouching, lurking, standing proud, being defiant, turning its back, gazing at the sky or huddling against the environment. This is because we use our social knowledge from interacting with other people as a tool to interpret our surroundings (see *Identity*). In the same way that we interpret body posture and orientation to understand emotional states, relationships and potential actions of humans, we use the same knowledge to understand things that are not humans.

Human agency is a type of imagined action that is generally only possible to be performed by a person, or that we associate strongly with other humans (see *Implied Action*). Agency is the ability for some-thing to act in a situation, making a static object or space into an active participant in its context. When we give objects the ability to dance, embrace, hold, catch or carry, these are activities we associate with other people. Likewise, we might consider motion as a type of action if it affects its surroundings and forms can saunter, sprint, dawdle, walk determinately or stroll. Each of these actions have a character-istic formal composition which allows us to identify it as such – static gestures of wrapping arms or a series of vertical lines that have a sense of swaying to an imaginary rhythm. When we find these gestures in

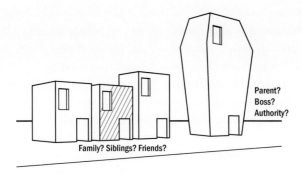

Parent?
Boss?
Authority?

Family? Siblings? Friends?

Human SOCIAL RELATIONS

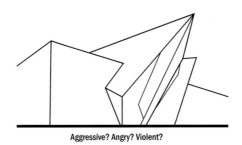

Aggressive? Angry? Violent?

Human EMOTIONAL STATES

the physical environment, we make an association between them and possible human experiences that might fit the context in order to determine what type of human agency (if any) might be present.

Human social relations could be considered as a type of agency as this personification gives objects the ability to affect their surroundings. However, where human agency implies direct, physical action, human social relations suggests that aspects of our environment operate in the same social structure as people and express social behaviours in the same way as us. This means that objects and spaces in our environment are given the ability to have family, friends, agreements, power structures and status through how we interpret their formal characteristics and spatial positioning. The basic information we use to understand social relations is proximity, similarity, orientation and projected attention (see *Relationship*). Things that are close to each other and physically similar suggest a type of social bond, such as siblings or close friends. Another type of social relation is based on status and authority when one aspect of the built environment is given influence, control, domination or power over other aspects of that same environment. Anytime we have a perceived difference in power between two or more objects, we have the introduction of hierarchy (see *Importance* and *Hierarchy*). Status and authority are generally connected to scale and spatial position with large, tall objects being more controlling than small and things that are up or above are seen has having power over those things below or under.

Once an object or space is considered to have the capacities of a person through actions and interactions, it should not be a surprise that we also consider them to have human emotional states. We can consider a thing that is not a person to be aggressive, restful, happy, silly, serious, sombre or harsh in the same way as people. We judge whether a human is happy, sad, angry or silly based on their facial expressions, clothing and body posture. For the built environment, we consider the shape, detail and qualities (materiality, colour, texture) of a location in the same way. A brightly coloured building is festive, a monochrome one with little detailing is sombre or reserved, a low-lit space is secretive and so on. It is our experience in our social and emotional context which provides the information to make these judgements.

Personification is an enrichment overlaid on other primary relationships and operates through speculation and suggestions that are both physically and culturally contextual. Even though they are based in the physical experience of our bodies, expressions of human emotional states, status and social interactions can change through context, fashion, norms, beliefs and local interpretation. As a designer, care should be taken not to consider personification in a literal way through symbolism or as a fixed set of universal rules. Human communication and interpretation operate through inference so it is possible to have the same form in two different contexts be understood in two different ways. While a symbol is a fixed relationship where one thing stands in for something else, personification is a gestural association using embodied concepts. This means that a form might have a range of possible interpretations while still having a major tendency supported by other aspects of the environment. A smile does not always mean someone is happy and we interpret the purpose of the expression by relating it to many other factors in that situation.

PROXIMITY

PROXIMITY IS SIMPLY HOW CLOSE something is to something else. While the idea might seem simple, it turns out to be very important because humans understand that things within the reach of our arms can be touched or held. The possibility of physical contact then means that we can manipulate, affect, control, influence, understand or accept the thing in close proximity to us. Since one of the ways people understand our environment is by projecting our own experiences and values into it, we give things around us the same abilities as people based on proximity (see *Personification*). Something close to us can affect us through real or perceived touch. Something that touches us is a thing that either we should pay attention to or something that can influence us – it is some sort of relationship. The relationship might take on many forms including benign, positive, caring, detrimental or abusive but, regardless, relative distance is one way that we understand a relationship to be present (see *Relationship*). Things near us can affect us because we give them the power to do so. The reverse is also true – the further away something is from us, we have less concern about it as we consider it outside our ability to influence and we are outside its ability to directly affect us. This makes proximity a bi-directional idea. We use relative distance between things to understand more complex concepts such as presence, belonging, authority, power and influence.

In formal environments, we interpret objects and surfaces as having influence and effect on each other based on proximity. This relationship might not include a person directly, but it will always be from a

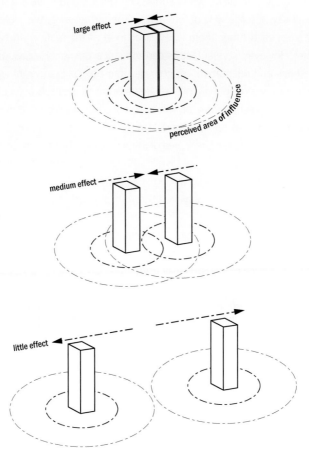

Proximity (RELATIVE ADJACENCY)

human viewpoint. When objects are close, they have *adjacency* (we use the term *adjoining* when addressing spaces) and there is a high possibility of some type of interaction. The further away two objects are from each other, there is less likelihood of them affecting each other. However, several factors can influence proximity – including presence and orientation. We consider that objects in environments project outwards to influence an area around them. Each object we perceive is given an area of influence based on its presence in the environment (see *Presence* and *Identity*). A presence that is more prominent will have a larger area of influence and objects with strong presence can be further away while still creating proximity (this is the same area of effect created through *Centrality*).

Proximity is not just achieved through physical characteristics as we often use sight to stand in for touch. We can create perceived closeness or even touch through interpreting something as looking at something else with a focused gaze. For people, our eyes are understood as a force extending away from our bodies that makes a physical connection between the origin of vision and the point of focus (as in "she pinned me with her gaze"). It works the same way with objects but since objects cannot really see anything, gaze and sight are formal interpretations – we map the shape of something to other types of information. The orientation of the object becomes important as gaze is projected from what we consider to be front of objects and front will, therefore, have a larger area of influence than other sides (see *Front* and *Orientation*). The more intense the interpretation of the projected gaze, the stronger the sense of proximity is created through visual connection.

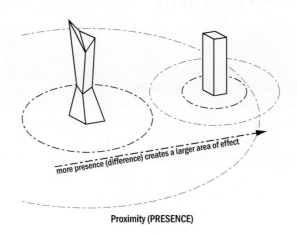

more presence (difference) creates a larger area of effect

Proximity (PRESENCE)

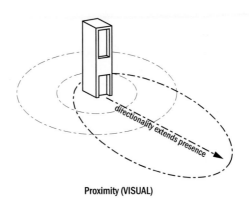

directionality extends presence

Proximity (VISUAL)

RELATIONSHIP

IT WOULD NOT SURPRISE ANYONE to be told that people have relationships with other people – which simply means that two or more people have some sort of association that affects the way they interact and how they behave to each other. It would also not surprise anyone to be told that people develop relationships with things other than people – be it a pet, a car, a house, some electronic device or some part of the environment such as a favourite vista, a nook in a coffee shop or a neighbourhood tree. We build these relationships by projecting human capacities, actions and abilities into things that are not human. We also believe that two or more things that are not human to have relationships independent to us (or so we think). Buildings facing each other can be *yelling*, *chatting* or *whispering* across a dividing street, trees can *huddle* together, two monuments in a city *claim* a space between them, benches can *crowd* a plaza and similar doors, buildings or cities can be *siblings*. None of these things are factual – those relationships do not actually exist outside of human interpretation. However, since people project these relationships onto objects, they are psychologically real because they have an effect.

Every relationship that we perceive in the environment has its basis in the interpersonal interactions between people and other people. As social beings, we are used to interpreting how someone is feeling towards us; if someone is friendly, affectionate, wary or hostile. While we listen for tone of voice and the words they use, we also take in a large amount of information from the shape of someone's body and their position in space relative to us. We look for clues in this physical and

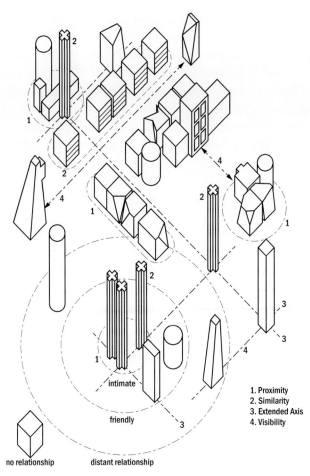

intimate

friendly

distant relationship

no relationship

1. Proximity
2. Similarity
3. Extended Axis
4. Visibility

Relationships in Formal Environments

spatial information to allow us to understand their attitude and mood towards us. We then use the same information to understand things that are not people. In architectural environments, the size, shape, texture, colour, spatial positioning, alignment and proximity of objects in space are the basis of interpreting the nature of relationships between objects and other objects. As a group of people standing very close together and leaning in can be understood as being intimate, so too a group of objects clustered together and angled towards each other, such as buildings or columns, are understood as having *the same type* of relationship.

The major concepts used to imply relationships between things in the built environment are proximity, similarity, extended axis and visibility. Physical attributes, such as colour and shape, contain important information for relationships although this is also related to the interpretation of an individual element in addition to the association of several elements together (see *Identity*). First, we must determine if a relationship is present, then we will look for characteristics that tell us the nature of that relationship.

Objects that are close or touching each other are usually interpreted as having a relationship (see *Proximity*). The opposite is also true, when something is far away from something else, this indicates a lack of relationship (although this can be modified by *visibility* or *similarity*). When objects get very close to each other, they can be understood as being parts of whole rather than individual elements. In architectural terms, this is useful for making several single buildings into complexes, surfaces of different shapes and colours into an integrated edge or to arrange fixtures or furnishings into understandable associations.

Similarity leads to the expectation of a relationship as things that look the same are grouped together conceptually (see *Similarity*). We do this with people – we expect family members to resemble each other or we understand cultural groups through ethnic identifiers such as hair or skin colour. We also do this with objects – whether buildings, building elements, furnishings, façades, other architectural elements or even the shape of spaces. A collection of similar buildings or spaces will create an association even if they are not close together. In context, similarity can often modify proximity as our ability to group like-with-like is a powerful conceptual organization tool.

Extended axis creates relationships through objects seeming to project into their environment along imaginary lines (see *Directionality*). When we interpret an extended axis to be present, objects on that axis will be associated with each other. A series of columns in a grid is an example of relationship through extended axis, even if the grid is not regular.

Visibility is important for people and our natural tendency is to build relationships with things that we can see and those that can see us. In architectural terms, this makes a front important as we understand it as the primary plane of engagement (see *Orientation*, *Front* and the visual aspect of *Proximity*). Any element in the perceived gaze of another will be considered as part of a relationship. This is how two monumental buildings in a city perceived to face each other, even across some considerable distance, are understood as having a relationship.

Once there is a relationship determined to exist, we will then start to consider the nature of that relationship. This is complex information, affected by context and operating through projecting human characteristics into non-human things (see *Personification*).

SPATIAL QUALITY

A SPATIAL QUALITY IS ANY attribute or characteristic connected to a space that can be described. Each space has multiple qualities associated with the objects, surfaces and natural phenomena present there. The combination of individual spatial qualities forms the overall character of the space. Basic attributes come from visual information as such as scale, volume, materiality, physical ordering, surface shapes and spatial ratio (width, height and length relationship). We also interpret qualities from environmental characteristics through sight and hearing (light, view, sound), sensory information from our skin (temperature, air pressure, air movement, humidity) and body senses (elevation, balance). Spaces have qualities because people perceive them as having qualities, making the notion a judgement. When we enter a space, we take in its qualities to form our impression of the character of the space. The measure of this interpretation is our bodies and our experiences.

Although character is subjective, it is also a shared experience. We can agree that a space can be described in the same way by many people. This might be cosy, expansive, exposed, harsh, airy, formal, casual or intimate – terms which summarize the various attributes present into an overall expression. None of these terms are good or bad statements but only descriptions. Whether the space is successful or not depends on how the overall quality supports the context and experiential needs of the user. We use spatial quality as the primary type of information to understand formal identity (see *Identity* and *Personification*), define patterns (see *Pattern* and *Type*), affect formal decisions (see *Force*) and organize spatialized events (see *Program*).

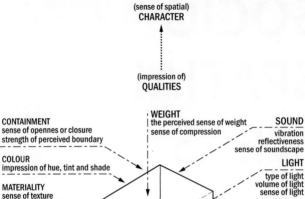

(sense of spatial)
CHARACTER

(impression of)
QUALITIES

CONTAINMENT
sense of openness or closure
strength of perceived boundary

COLOUR
impression of hue, tint and shade

MATERIALITY
sense of texture
sense of durability

EXPOSURE
sense of visual accessibility
visual openness/vista
sense of exposure

CONNECTEDNESS
sense of physical accessibility
sense of connectedness
accessible or defensive

WEIGHT
the perceived sense of weight
sense of compression

SOUND
vibration
reflectiveness
sense of soundscape

LIGHT
type of light
volume of light
sense of light

VOLUME
type and scale of convexity
ratio between dimensions
sense of enclosure

degree of publicness
degree of privacy

SHAPE
impression of surface form
cultural associations

QUALITIES related to Physical Environments

MAKING ARCHITECTURE THROUGH BEING HUMAN

SOCIO-SPATIAL IDEAS

PEOPLE HAVE A SPECIAL RELATIONSHIP with space. While humans are very fond of objects and our individual experience with them as negotiated from our centres (our directional bodies), one of the most important aspects of our lives is the space between those objects. The act of living our lives centres on the experience of moving through and performing activities in spaces. More importantly, the spaces in which we exist are also the locations we *negotiate our relationships with other people*. This is significant as it activates the spaces around us with a series of spatialized ideas that are based on human social values, needs and relations.

Human spaces are shaped through architectural intention to support the needs of people. While many of these needs are physiological – about shelter, warmth, light and fresh air – many others are about more abstract things such as safety, belonging and esteem. Things in this latter group are not directly quantifiable as they exist only as agreements between people. However, these ideas do affect architecture through the shaping, composition and sequencing of spaces. When architects associate a series of voids together, this is done to support different types of human activities, social exposure, perceptions of safety, degrees of privacy and ease of accessibility – all ideas that are social but manifest through formal content. This section addresses ideas focusing on the relation of one bounded space to another and the social information they contain. Some of the ideas build from formal concepts and situated notions but the focus shifts from object to objectified space.

COMMUNALITY

COMMUNALITY IS THE DEGREE of socialness of a space. It is not the space itself that is social but the types of activities of people that take place in that space. Spaces with communality are those that encourage social interaction between the occupants – they are spaces where people come together. Social spaces can be either public or private (see *Privacy*) as well as highly connected or isolated (see *Connectedness*) while still being communal. This is because while privacy is about controlling exposure and connectedness is about the ability to move, communality is how a space supports gathering. In communal spaces, the formal arrangement of surfaces to contain voids is focused on orientating human bodies towards each other. If connectedness is a line (see *Axis*), communality is a circle (see *Convexity*).

A library and a coffee shop are both spaces where people gather – they are building types designed to support the interaction between people. Both spaces have few restrictions to enter so lean towards publicness, require a sense of presence in their context and are highly connected. However, a library and a coffee shop have different degrees of communality, different patterns of convexity and different tolerances to activities. A traditional library, as a collector and disseminator of knowledge, is based on moments of gathering arranged to minimize physical activities and sound. These convexities generally have a small radius and are arranged with thresholds between them (see *Threshold*) or isolated so to decrease conflict between events such as talking or reading (i.e. the convexities are low density). In contrast,

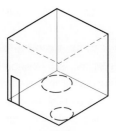

Areas supporting gathering in a
LOW-DENSITY COMMUNAL space
(i.e. library)

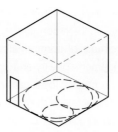

Areas supporting gathering in a
HIGH-DENSITY COMMUNAL space
(i.e. coffeeshop)

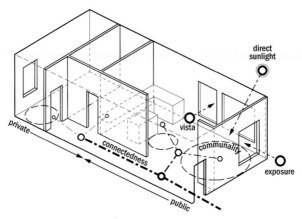

Spaces with HIGH COMMUNALITY INDEPENDENT to connectedness and privacy
(i.e. single family house)

the coffee shop is highly communal as it supports social interaction to a larger degree, and can tolerate more activity, sound and events. The convexities are more closely packed with less threshold space (i.e. the convexities are high density).

An example of communality familiar to most can be found in the arrangement, quality and operation of spaces in a single-family house. The entrance foyer, hall and parts of main living area are highly connected spaces and the most public; other parts of the living room, the dining room and kitchen are less connected and semi-public. The bedrooms are the least connected and the most private. However, the most communal of the five spaces is the living room followed by the dining room. If there is an area or nook within a bedroom meant for sitting and visiting, this also has communality while being highly private. The need for communality in these spaces are supported by other spatial qualities reinforcing the casual and relaxed discussion of the living room and the single convexity arranged around the activity of eating in the dining room. These include light quality, light source, exposure, vista and a sense of shelter through implied containment.

There is an inverse relationship between communality and movement (see *Path-Goal*, *Journey* and *Procession*). Where a path is a line that facilitates the movement of a body and encourages those activities that require a changed location of the body in each moment, communality is a circle that contains the body in a static location so to build a longer-term relationship with other bodies. This means that paths should be adjacent to communal spaces, touching but not penetrating. When a path does enter a communal space, it either suppresses the intended activity through its proximity or creates two gathering spaces instead of one. Movement (path, axis) and convexity need to support but not interfere with each other.

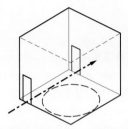

Circulation adjacent to convex gathering space

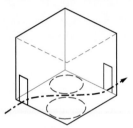

The introduction of circulation through a convex space suppresses
large scale communality and generates smaller gathering possibilities

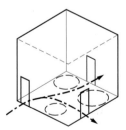

As circuation becomes more dominant,
the possible scale of gathering decreases

Communality and CIRCULATION

CONNECTEDNESS

CONNECTEDNESS IS THE WAY spaces are related in terms of physical access – how one space allows entry to another and how many spaces are connected to that one space. The simple question that addresses connectedness is "where does this space allow me to get to?". If the answer is something like "quite a lot of other places", then that space is highly connected. While the question is simple, the idea has a significant role to play in our experience of the built environment. This is because connectedness is about human movement, accessibility and choices – all events that affect our social engagement of space. The primary ordering principles associated with connectedness are the axis and the node (see *Axis* and *Radiosity*).

When we move through space, that movement allows us to access other places, people and things. It allows gathering and socialization but also encourages discovery through exposure, visibility and procession. These are human ideas and human events that form human relationships supported by the arrangement and relationships between spaces. Spaces that are highly integrated (i.e. connected or linked together) with each other also tend to be highly social because of the ease of access and the degree of exposure. In this way, social interactions between people are supported by spatial composition through ideas of path, journey, visibility and procession.

Highly connected spaces are often highly public but not always (see *Privacy*). Spaces such as lobbies, streets, atriums and forecourts have a strong degree of connectedness. They are spaces that allow access to many other types of spaces and are highly integrated as

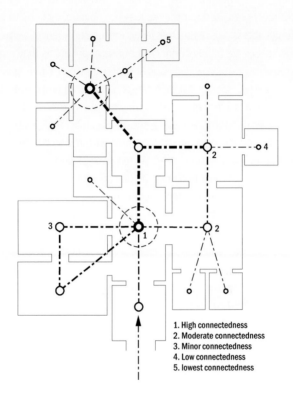

1. High connectedness
2. Moderate connectedness
3. Minor connectedness
4. Low connectedness
5. lowest connectedness

Connectedness and SPATIAL INTEGRATION

they link several sequences of spaces together. They also have few restrictions to entry and an ambiguous sense of ownership which encourages us to define them as public. However, a space might still be strongly connected to other spaces but have restrictions to entry that limits access. Spaces such as living rooms, conference rooms and lounge spaces are highly connected but semi-private as they require membership in the particular social group that owns that space in order to gain access, be it a member of a family, an employee at the company, or a student at a school. Truly private spaces tend towards a low degree of connectedness as the ideas conflict with each other.

Connectedness has a direct association with the architectural idea of circulation. Circulation is the directed flow of people through an environment such as a building. Circulation introduces paths based on the logic and relationships between spaces that suggest how someone should move through that environment, what spaces they might visit and in which order that should occur (see *Path-Goal*, *Journey* and *Procession*). Most environments have several circulation patterns arranged in a hierarchy, addressing the major flows of people as an experience. Circulating spaces are those spaces that are primarily defined for the activity of movement – corridors, stairs, elevators, lobbies and foyers. These spaces also support the idea of connectedness as they tend to be spaces that are used to connect other spaces. Circulation spaces are axial and when axes meet at a centre (i.e. a node), they connect that centre to whatever occurs at the other end of the axis. The more axes that meet at a centre, the higher the degree of connectedness of that centre.

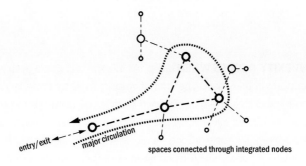

spaces connected through integrated nodes

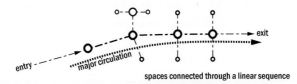

spaces connected through a linear sequence

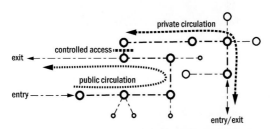

spaces connected to two types of ownership
producing two different primary circulations

Connectedness and CIRCULATION

CONVEXITY

CONVEXITY OCCURS WHEN any point in a space is visible from any other point in that space. The limit of visibility makes a boundary. As a geometrical idea, the space defined by these points tends towards roundness. Circles, squares, spheres and cubes all have strong convexity while a line or extruded shape with a long axis has little to no convexity. For architecture, convexity is a social idea as points in space are also the possible location of people. When people gather in a space, they move into positions where they can be aware, see and interact with others. This means we tend to make a circle through the arrangement of our bodies – a shape with strong convexity that supports co-presence and co-awareness through its formal geometry.

If we gather to interact socially without a structured hierarchy (i.e. there is no social authority or focal point), this is supported by spaces which are highly convex and without directionality. It is one of the reasons why a discussion of equals is often situated around a round table, or a social gathering that is based in small discussions between multiple people operates best in a square room. The convexity of the space allows the social event of human discussion to occur more easily. However, the moment we introduce some form of hierarchy – a speaker, a presentation, a performance, a head table and so on – the space needs some form of directionality which tends to shift the spatial composition away from convexity (see *Directionality* and *Pattern*). As directionality increases and convexity decreases (i.e. the space becomes less round and more linear), we shift from supporting gathering to implying movement.

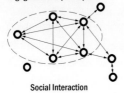

convex space created through all participants being able to engage all other participants

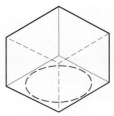

Social Interaction

Formal Manifestation

CONVEXITY

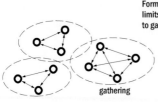

Formal composition limits ability to gather

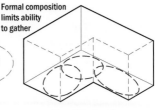

gathering

Social Interaction

Formal Manifestation

Convexity in CONCAVE SPACE

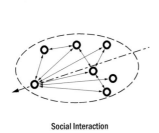

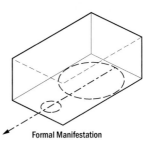

Social Interaction

Formal Manifestation

Convexity with DIRECTIONALITY

EVENT AFFINITY

EVENT AFFINITY IS WHEN two or more events that take place in adjacent spaces are compatible with each other. An event is something that occurs in a particular place for some length of time. When events have affinity, the physical effects of one event does not interfere and may even improve the experience of the adjacent event. The lack of event affinity causes conflict and decreased success for all adjacent events. It is an idea that has a major impact of spatial arrangement and formal composition. Imagine you are studying for an exam and there are two friends nearby. One of them is playing loud music while doing cartwheels while the other is making a sandwich. These three different events need different formal compositions with different spatial qualities to be successful (see *Spatial Quality*). Each event also projects into the surrounding environment the outcome of its activity – it has a presence. Studying and making food have a closer affinity as they share more common characteristics and have little presence beyond a small area-of-effect. Neither generates much noise while both need spaces that support a small range of motion and focused task lighting. As spatialized events, these two can be placed near each other without one interfering with the other (neutral affinity). The cartwheel event requires very different spatial qualities to support its activity and generates outcomes which are incompatible with studying (negative affinity). None of the three events are yet conceived as being beneficial for each other as the proximity of one does not raise the experiential value of another (positive affinity).

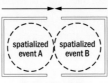

Spaces with affinity

Spaces without affinity (SPATIAL DISTANCE)

Spaces without affinity (FORMAL INTERVENTION)

Event Affinity and PROXIMITY

At a basic level, event affinity is associated with how close and visible one space can be to another depending on what occurs in those spaces (see *Connectedness*, *Exposure* and *Procession*). If we do not have an option to separate events through distance, then some type of formal intervention is needed to negotiate the relationship between events in adjacent spaces. The type of intervention will differ depending if the events have positive, neutral or negative affinities for each other. Positive affinities would look for formal ways to associate the events together through location and view while still allowing both events to occur without interruption. Negative affinity would look for formal ways to isolate, mediate and suppress the projected outcomes from the events so they do not interfere with each other. Since events are human activities, they are also dynamic – which means that time and duration play a part in event affinity. Some events might not be compatible with each other in the moment they occur but have strong affinity through shared spatial needs. For example, a lunchroom and a gymnasium in a school typology (see *Type*) require a similar scale, convexity and connectedness. Museum galleries hold positive values to double as reception gathering locations (i.e. wedding, corporate fundraiser) as they share convexity, scale and cultural identity values. When the qualities associated with one spatialized event benefits the needs of another event, those event might overlap (intersection), interlace or even merge (addition) *if* those two events do not occur at the same time and the individual identity needs can be resolved while reinforcing a shared space (see *Identity*).

An architectural designer will resolve affinity between spatialized events using location, connectedness, proximity, formal characteristics, spatial quality and formal intervention. The goal is to allow all events to not only co-exist successfully but also add value to each other in some way. One of the main applications of event affinity is through program resolution (see *Program*).

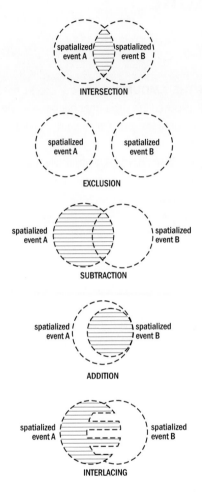

Spatial Relationships through FORMAL OPERATIONS

EXPOSURE

EXPOSURE IS THE AMOUNT of sensory access between spaces. Spaces that are exposed are those that are open to view from other spaces through sightlines, open to sound through openings and vibration transfer or open to smell through air circulation. These points of exposure do not have to be physically accessible to a human body, which makes this idea complementary but different to those ideas that address access between spaces based on movement (see *Connectedness* and *Procession*). Rather, the presentation of a space visually to its surroundings or the allowance of sound or smell trans-mission is a parallel factor in architectural quality and success. Spaces that are exposed allow themselves to be more public and reduce the barriers of control in order to gain some benefit or need for the activ-ities contained within that space.

There are many variations and degrees of exposure. There are also overlaps between one type of exposure and another. Where a void or opening might provide physical access to a space, it might also provide visual access or acoustic transparency. Another situation might have one space visually accessible but physically and auditorily separate while another might allow the transmission of sound but is isolated to view and movement. The spatial qualities of exposure are variable because they need to be determined by the contextual needs of the space and the types of events it supports. Exposure can be positive when it aligns with the needs of a human event or nega-tive when it interferes with those needs.

Visual exposure occurs when it is possible to see into one space from another. This type of exposure sets up a relationship between

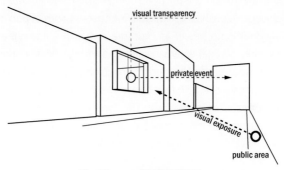

Visual Exposure (HIERARCHICAL)

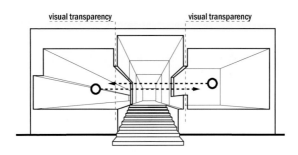

Visual Exposure (MUTUAL)

things that do not physically touch nor are part of a path or sequence. Visual exposure might be a mutual event with two spaces able to see into each other or it might include hierarchy where one space is clearly the viewer and the other is the thing being viewed (see *Personification*). Hierarchical relationships in exposure introduces issues of publicness, privacy, control and power as exposure reveals the internal events of a space into a larger external realm (see *Privacy*). While things that are highly exposed tend towards being highly public, it is possible to expose private events into a public space if that type of visibility benefits both spaces in some way. The common occurrence of visual exposure is using large windows, balconies, landings and mezzanines to allow the events of one space to be visually experienced by an adjacent space but without physical connection.

Other categories of exposure include sound and scents – types of sensory information that are often attempted to be reduced, minimized or eliminated in interaction between spaces in our built environment. However, isolation should not always be assumed as there are situations where sound or scent will introduce an important or positive effect. The burble of moving water, the hum of voices that elicits activity or the aroma of food are all positive sensory experiences that can enrich an architectural space. In these cases, it is important to determine what the effect should be, who should have access to this effect, and how the formal environment should respond physically to support that exposure.

While exposure is a different idea to connectedness and procession, it can be used to activate journey. When one space is exposed to another and the effect is desirable, it becomes a destination even if the path to that goal is not directly visible. We will start to look for a way to achieve our destination through environmental clues.

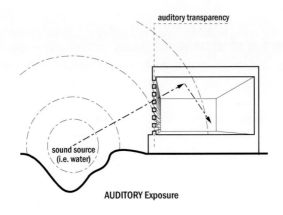

AUDITORY Exposure

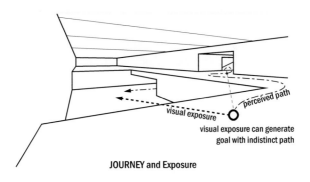

visual exposure can generate
goal with indistinct path

JOURNEY and Exposure

FORCE

A FORCE IS SOMETHING that makes something else happen. In architectural design, a force is any non-formal event that causes a formal reaction. A non-formal event is simply something that occurs, exists or happens in the world but is not an object (i.e. does not have a solid physical form). It might be a natural phenomenon or event but can also be human interactions, needs, desires or beliefs. The idea of forces is used to make compositional, orientational and material decisions that are highly relevant to their context by allowing the event to cause a response or change in the physical (formal) composition of an environment. Primary forces in architecture fall into the categories of environmental, individual body (ergonomic), multiple bodies (social) and cultural (identity).

The easiest forces to identify and use are those that can be conceptualized as an object or substance (see *Objectification*). Environmental forces such as sunlight, wind, gravity or precipitation can be understood in this way. We can consider sunlight as a force by conceptualizing it as a series of parallel lines that travel from the sun to our position on the surface of the Earth. We think of those lines as a physical object which have definable properties such altitude, azimuth angle and illumination. When we consider the effect of that object on the placement of surfaces (to block light) and openings (to allow light to pass through), we have turned light into a force as it causes a change in the form. In the same way, placing surfaces to block a strong current of air, creating a sloped plane above our heads to shelter from the rain, using a rise in the ground to achieve a

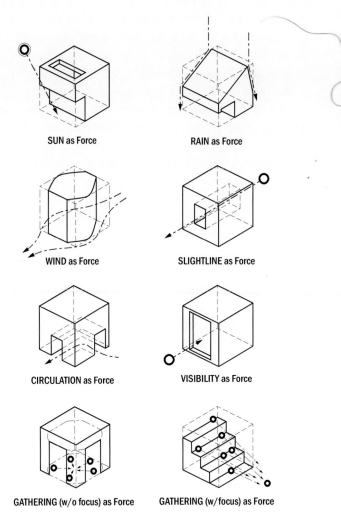

SUN as Force

RAIN as Force

WIND as Force

SLIGHTLINE as Force

CIRCULATION as Force

VISIBILITY as Force

GATHERING (w/o focus) as Force

GATHERING (w/focus) as Force

view, thinking about structure as pushing up against a heavy object or placing a dense surface between a loud space and a quiet space to suppress noise are all translations of non-formal events to affect formal design. In these cases, we are using wind, precipitation, topography, gravity and sound as forces.

The needs of our bodies and our interaction with other people can also be understood as forces by thinking about them as objects, substances and pressures. The most common body and social information affecting formal composition are those connected to movement, sight, communality (sociability) and privacy. When movement is used as a force, we can think about it as a substance. It can be used to place surfaces and voids in support of how people are expected to flow through an area. As a force, movement will affect the placement of walls and circulation elements (stairs, ramps, elevators), the materiality of surfaces, and the placement of openings to allow or restrict physical access and exposures. In the same way, when form is arranged to allow for a sightline through or from a location, sight is being used as force to create a void for view.

Social events can also be considered as forces that affect the arrangement of the formal environment. The social situations of people standing in a line, gathering as a large group to listen to a speaker, or gathering in small groups to talk to each other each contain non-formal information that can be understood as a force. This includes how people are expected to interact with each other, what they are focused on, what they should be able to see and hear, the quantity of people in the space and how long the event lasts. The different social interactions in each of the situations generate different formal responses *if* we consider the role of the built environment is to support human events. People arranged front-to-back facing one direction generates a formal response of line where the gathering of people supports a formal response of circle (see *Axis* and *Convexity*). In the situation of gathering to listen to a speaker, there is little to no expected social interaction between people in the audience with each other but there is a high degree of relationship between each audience member and the speaker. The view lines between all members of the audience and the presenter can be thought of as a force. The need to hear the presentation as clearly as possible can also be understood as a force. This creates a particular response in the formal arrangement of the space – one that arranges multiple seating locations with a view to a single focal point in a convex space with strong directionality. In contrast, when we have a small group gathering, considering social interactions and needs as forces creates a series of smaller, sheltered convex spaces with good containment, no directionality and a sense of intimacy.

Since a force can be generated from any non-formal event, this can include less clearly defined information such as memory, identity, desire, affection and status. These are less easily understood as objects but can be conceptualized as a pressure or influence. We use memory as a force when we create shapes that reference historical periods to transfer the socio-political values from that previous time to our current environment. We use identity as a force when we select particular materials, program elements and colours that respond to values held by the inhabitants of that space. Almost any event has the potential of being used as a force *as long as that information can generate a formal response* and that response is deemed relevant to its context.

INTERIORITY

INTERIORITY IS THE EXPERIENCE of being within something. It comes from how we think of our body as a container with an inside and outside. The things "inside" our bodies are our thoughts which include emotions, feelings and desires. The things "outside" our bodies are known through our senses and include our environment and other people. When we shift our awareness from our *external* senses to our *internal* sensations to focus on the working of our mind, this is an act of interiority. Interiority is connected to other ideas through this experience. Since our thoughts are known only by us until we release them outside our body through some expression or communication, we understand the experience of interiority as being private. We also decide what thoughts should be exposed and when that might happen, relating interiority to ideas of control. Control, in turn, is closely connected to issues of safety. These are important and fundamental things for people.

While interiority starts with the negotiation between internal thoughts and external experiences, we extend the idea to interpret the experiences of our body in social environments – how we interact with other people and how that is supported through particular locations and compositions. This means that the physical objects, shapes and details that make up our built environment can help or inhibit relationships between people. Interiority introduces a sense of containment that brings the benefits of shelter, safety, inclusion and privacy (see *Containment*). It follows that exteriority as the opposite

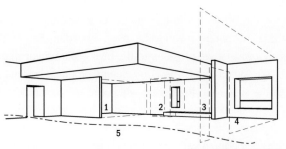

Sense of interiority created by:
1. Corner containment
2. Protected visibility out
3. Edge containment
4. No interiority (exposed – visual)
5. No interiority (exposed – motion)

Interiority in INTERIOR SPACE

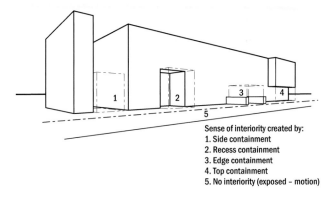

Sense of interiority created by:
1. Side containment
2. Recess containment
3. Edge containment
4. Top containment
5. No interiority (exposed – motion)

Interiority in EXTERIOR SPACE

idea of being outside introduces publicness, presence, separation and exposure.

Interiority is not tied to the perimeter of a building or the front door. It does not simply mean to be inside a building. Rather, interiority is an *idea* that we project into the built environment through a perceived containment. The containment produces an intimacy between the space and the person which also allows the person to control their relationship with other people (see *Exposure*). A space with four walls, a floor and a roof may not express interiority as strongly as a condition with simply two walls. A sense of interiority is highly contextual and has much to do with the contrast between that moment and its adjacencies as well as the perceived qualities of those spaces. A courtyard may produce interiority without being enclosed where a glass fronted office lobby may not. This is because the courtyard actively isolates space while a lobby actively connects to adjacent spaces through visibility. A recessed doorway on a busy street can be a moment of interiority if a person uses it to step out of the flow of the crowd and collect their thoughts. While we would not consider the recess of a door as "inside", it produces a very different quality of space to the street immediately next to it. Interiority occurs because we consider the door recess to be a "slower" and more protective space in contrast with the "fast" space of the exposed, linear, highly public street.

Interiority as a spatial moment allows a person to remove their attention from their surroundings, to feel safe, and to feel in control. It is produced through arranging surfaces to form spaces that give the sense of separation and privacy. These spaces are usually scaled to relate directly to the human body, often smaller in contrast to adjacent spaces.

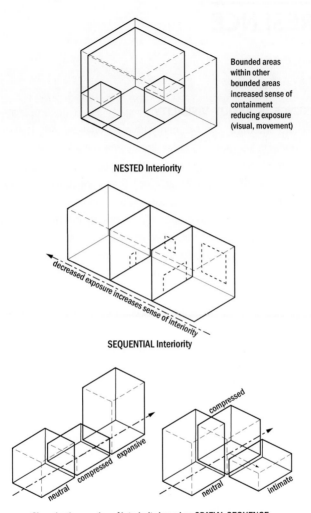

Bounded areas
within other
bounded areas
increased sense of
containment
reducing exposure
(visual, movement)

NESTED Interiority

decreased exposure increases sense of interiority

SEQUENTIAL Interiority

neutral compressed expansive

compressed

neutral intimate

Changing Impression of Interiority based on SPATIAL SEQUENCE

PRESENCE

PRESENCE IS ABOUT VISIBILITY. It starts as an uncomplicated idea that something can be seen within an environment, but this idea connects to more complex social interpretations. When we notice something, we bring our attention to bear on that thing (see *Importance*). As the physical nature of that thing becomes more prominent to our attention through scale, material or position, we understand it to have more presence. Presence creates hierarchy as it arranges our attention in terms of what we will pay attention to first (see *Hierarchy*). It creates order through becoming a focal point of a centre or terminated axis (or making a centre and starting an axis). While presence is *possible* when we see something, it only *occurs* when we interpret the thing being seen as actively extending itself into the surrounding environment (see *Force*). In the same way we under-stand the presence of a person as the projection of intangibles such as their personality, values and character outwards from their centre through representative surfaces (i.e. their body, face and clothes), we also interpret the surfaces of an object, such as a building or wall, as projecting outwards into its context. Objects with strong presence are understood by us to have a large effect on their environment through this perceived outwards projection that activates the social ideas of quality, status and influence.

Presence might start with visibility but is really about effect and significance. When people have presence, they can influence the behaviour of other people around them. When objects in environ-ments have presence, we give them the same ability to influence

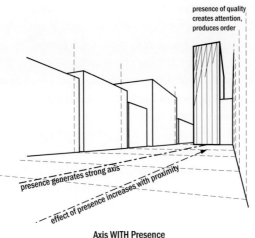

presence of quality creates attention, produces order

presence generates strong axis

effect of presence increases with proximity

Axis WITH Presence

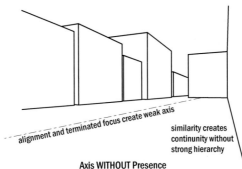

alignment and terminated focus create weak axis

similarity creates continunity without strong hierarchy

Axis WITHOUT Presence

things around them. This means that presence is a type of agency based on force of personality rather than implied action or motion (see *Personification* and *Identity*). A building or surface with presence creates an area of effect surrounding it that marks influence and determines the outer edge of possible relationships. This might be a field or territory centred on the object and extending in all directions if there is significant difference in scale or a direct line of view between the object and context (see *Centrality*). It might also be directional and project outwards from a surface in one direction (see *Directionality*). The result is the attraction of *positive* attention that gives the object or surface a degree of social agency.

Not all objects, surfaces or spaces do or should have presence. Some buildings and rooms need to reduce their presence to be successful in their role. These situations use formal design decisions that lessen prominence, create similarity, decrease contrast or visual complexity of surfaces. Our interpretation of presence is tied to spatial and material quality as well as the formal relationship of the object in its context. Where a well-detailed façade using high quality materials at the end of a terminated vista (focus point of an axis) will create presence, a façade that continues an established rhythm, creates similarity through material and detailing and aligns with the scale of the context will reduce presence (see *Object-Ground*). Things we find in the environment might also have more presence than the built objects we situate around them. A significant tree, a unique rock outcropping or a picturesque pond can all be used to organize and focus the built environment in their context by extending their experiential quality. Ultimately, presence is an ordering principle but uses more complex social and cultural identity information that we project onto formal relationships.

Centre WITHOUT presence (similarity)

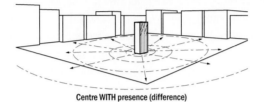

Centre WITH presence (difference)

RADIAL Presence

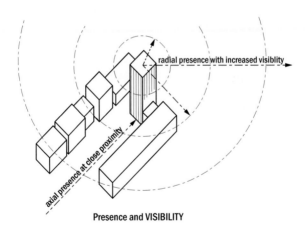

radial presence with increased visiblity

axial presence at close proximity

Presence and VISIBILITY

PRIVACY

PRIVACY IS THE ABILITY to be alone, the capacity to exist without intrusion into our thoughts or presence by others, the ability to control our body and the power to feel as if we are making decisions for ourselves without interference. We understand privacy as to be outside the influence of others. It is a social idea for without other people, there would be no need for the idea of privacy – we would always be alone. Our most private space is inside our own heads and there is a strong relationship between privacy and being within something as it relates to control (see *Interiority*). The other side to privacy is publicness. Publicness is the ability to be *present* in relation to other people. When we are public, we make ourselves available to be seen, engaged, interacted and interfered with as a choice. We give up some control for the benefits that comes with access to other people and locations. Publicness allows us to be influenced and we have limits placed on our behaviours and activities as we conform to social expectations.

While privacy and publicness are ideas about social interaction between people, the concepts have spatial implications as our environment can either support our need for privacy or give us access to publicness through how forms and spaces are arranged. This is because one of our basic interpretation of privacy and publicness is through how close something is to us (see *Proximity*) and how visible we are to others (see *Exposure*). These are events that can be affected by how we shape and organize spaces.

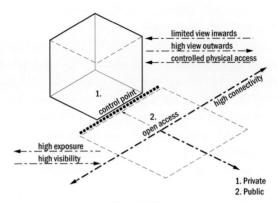

limited view inwards
high view outwards
controlled physical access

high connectivity

1.
control point

2.
open access

high exposure
high visibility

1. Private
2. Public

Private–Public

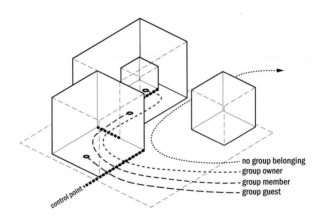

no group belonging
group owner
group member
group guest

control point

Privacy and BELONGING

In the built environment, spaces that encourage privacy are those that allow us to decide what physical and emotional experiences may occur to us. When we move into a form – put a wall between us and others, enter an enclosed space, walk into a depression in the ground – the surfaces act to shield our bodies from sight of others, to reduce exposure to noise and to remove ourselves from the ability to be touched. The spaces encourage us to believe we can control our interactions and limit external things that might influence us – factors that increase in our sense of privacy. Privacy produces a sense of safety through this feeling of managing contact with other people. At the same time, we can increase our perception of control if we can gather information about our surroundings without exposing ourselves. This is the ability to see without being seen and allows us to make decisions without outside influence or social pressure.

Publicness, in contrast, is about spaces that support interactions with others in ways that are less scripted. These are locations that are highly connected with reduced barriers to access (see *Connectedness*) and designed for gathering through scale, shape and materiality (see *Convexity*). They are spaces that tend towards a strong sense of shared identity, stressing cultural values over those of the individual (see *Identity*). Public spaces are locations where we, as individuals, abandon our own personal sense of control and ownership for the benefits of sharing, surprise, unanticipated activities and unscripted events – all which bring a value and richness to a human life.

Public and private space ultimately address issues of belonging and the right of access. While private space trends towards smaller, more intimate and more secure spaces (i.e. the windowless room) and public spaces trend towards large, open and exposed spaces (i.e. the field), the real test of if a space is public or private has to do with range of different social groups that may access that space without restriction. This is harder to quantify through spatial characteristics but does have a relationship to how spaces are connected to each other. One way to determine if a space is public or private is to identify who might enter the space without challenge, barrier to movement or restriction of use. A space with a degree of privacy is one that limits access to a select group or individual where a public space allows free access without challenge or restriction. If you arrive at the front door of a house with no relationship to the people who live there, you cannot just walk through that door. This is because residential space is private and restricted to a small group of people. As a guest in a residence, there is a social relationship that allows access but it is not unlimited. You might feel comfortable in the living room or dining room (semi-public), less so in the kitchen (sometimes more private) but an intruder in the bedroom (private). An employee of a business can enter through the front door without challenge but perhaps cannot enter certain rooms freely such as an administrator's office. Those rooms have a higher degree of privacy.

It is hard to find a space that is purely public or fully private as this idea exists as a gradient rather than an absolute. Understanding spatial access and belonging through the social relationship of the people existing in or visiting that location is a critical idea used for the arrangement and association of spaces to each other.

PROCESSION

PROCESSION IS THE ARRANGEMENT of voids to create a sequence of spatial experiences. When spaces are carefully considered in their relation to each other along a path, this is procession. A space not yet reached might presence on earlier locations in the sequence, or the experience of a space in which we have just arrived might be affected by where we have just been. We might think about procession simply as a path that connects a series of spaces together (see *Path-Goal* and *Journey*), but this would only be partly true. Procession is an aspect of journey, but its focus is on the shifting position and focus of human sensory experience rather than static formal relationships. Where journey can be understood in axonometric or plan, procession is understood as perspective. As an idea in architectural design, procession is an ordering principle that uses scripted human events based on movement and spatial composition to provide an intended experience.

Motion is the primary activator of procession as without the ability to change our location in space, we could not experience a sense of connected spaces. Human motion, however, involves speeds and modes that range from fast, focused and directed movement to wandering, strolling, jogging, walking, sauntering and, finally, standing still. Each mode of motion has a purpose in procession and can be affected or encouraged by formal composition (see *Directionality*, *Implied Motion* and *Implied Action*). We find other sensory information supporting motion including sight, sound, balance, temperature perception and smell. The introduction of sightlines (see *Exposure*),

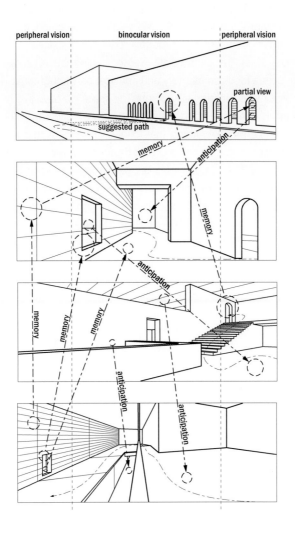

peripheral vision   binocular vision   peripheral vision

partial view

suggested path

memory   anticipation   memory

anticipation

memory   memory   memory

anticipation   anticipation

points of vista, shifting air quality, perceived containment, temperature variations and topographic slope affects the speed, mode and direction of our movement through a sequence of spaces.

More than just immediate sensory information, procession introduces a focus on memory and anticipation through time-based interactions and shifting viewpoints. The space we have just moved through is remembered as we enter the next space and influences how we interpret everything that follows. The spaces that we have not yet reached can be anticipated if those spaces are foreshadowed in some way. The glimpses of goals, partial views, obscured shapes, shadows and the slow revealing of elements can generate expectation for spaces not yet come. It is memory and anticipation as part of a scripted spatial experience that creates what we understand as spatial narrative. However, this type of narrative is very different to the general understanding of the term.

Spatial narrative can be described as *narrative-like* as it lacks many of the characteristics that makes something truly a story. A narrative requires several specific conditions to work – a fixed sequence of events arranged in time, a point of view (authorship), alignment with an overall purpose and the ability to control focus of the viewer (control exactly what someone is looking at). While procession is literally a connected series of spaces that orders human experience, that sequencing is not rigid, fixed or absolute. People can change their direction, stop in an area meant for movement, diverge from a path, and return from the way they came. Controlled focus is also not achievable as the gaze of the person in an environment is free to travel where it will without restriction. All procession can do is encourage the potential of experience through the thoughtful arrangement of spaces and formal elements. It introduces likely spatial sequences among many possibilities.

PROGRAM

A PROGRAM IS A CONTAINER that defines the scope of a project – usually a building or some other formalized space. The common form of a program is a list of room- or area-names and their associated sizes. However, a program is not the spaces themselves but the events that take place in those spaces. An event can range from basic actions such as sitting, gathering, storing, playing, cleaning, sleeping, eating, concentrating and relaxing to more complex socio-cultural actions and rituals that include events such as performance, debate, worship, study and negotiation. When several events are commonly found together, we identify their spatial location through a label or name as a quick way to reference those codified relationships. This is what we know as a room – a container or bounded area whose label stands in for all the normative events we would expect to find in that location without having to list each one separately. A bedroom is the label we give to a space in which we sleep but the activities in that space also include events of dressing, clothes storage, retreat, private workspace and possibly hygiene routines such as bathing and brushing your teeth. All the events of the bedroom share the need for privacy, decreased exposure, reduced communality and limited connectedness. They are also related in a time sequence and through human ritual – getting ready for bed, sleeping, intimacy and preparing for the day are events where one generally follows closely after the other, creating a pattern of human activity. While a room or area name might have a single name to identify it, it usually involves several events that have a high degree of affinity for each other.

When a program and its elements are deployed into physical space, it is an act of resolution and negotiation. Each program element (i.e. a room or bounded area) contains several events which need to be situated in relation to other program elements as well as events found in the surrounding built environment. This occurs by first understanding what spatial qualities that the events in the program need to be successful (see *Spatial Quality*). Does an event require a particular quality of light or view, exposure or isolation, a certain volume, or access to some other event through connection or proximity? The goal is a spatial resolution that allow each program element and its events to thrive while not interfering with any other event within its area of effect. In order to do this, we use affinities, opportunities and conflicts to identify possible adjacencies and spatialized relationships (see *Force* and *Event Affinity*). Events that need exposure and public visibility are attracted to locations in their context that provide these characteristics (fronts, public street or other areas of dense human activity). Events that require privacy need to be sheltered from highly public or highly exposed areas through either distance or formal intervention. Events that benefit from being next to each other can create larger groupings to share activities. Events that add quality to other events can create an attraction. Events that interfere with each other can be thought about as creating a repulsion that pushes them apart.

The act of programming is knowing what events are present but the act of program resolution is understanding the identity of each event, the nature of their container and their associations in order to determine how to resolve the need of that identity through spatial location, proximity, spatial quality and the formal arrangement of surfaces in space.

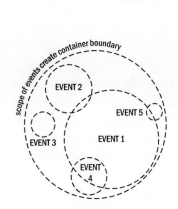

Room as CONTAINER FOR EVENTS

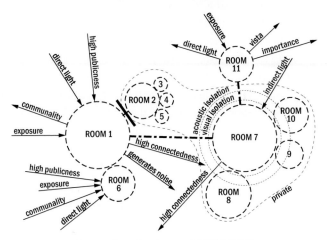

Program, Event Containers and EVENT AFFINITY

THRESHOLD

A THRESHOLD IS A CONDITION of being *between*. This condition brings opportunities and we understand it as a moment of transitioning from one experience to another, of making a decision, of committing to a path, and of being on the edge of something else. In architecture, the threshold is a physical volume of space that performs these actions. A porch is a threshold as it negotiates between the public space of the street and the private space of the house. A door is a threshold as it is a moment before we decide to enter. The primary purpose of a threshold is to allow a pause or reflection and mark a point of decision where we still have a choice to either go forward or return. A threshold creates a refuge through containment to allow this reflection to take place (see *Interiority*).

Thresholds can work as either a transition or buffer space depending on the events that are contained in the connecting spaces. As a transition, a threshold prepares a person for the next space in the sequence by relating the memory of previous space to the experience of the second space in a richer way (see *Procession*). As a buffer, the threshold operates to separate events that are disruptive to each other through some formal mechanism such as distance or compression (see *Event Affinity* and *Program*). In this way, a threshold space might be narrow or very deep, well-defined or gestural depending on its role in the relationship between the spaces it connects. Regardless, the identity of the threshold remains ambiguous, belonging neither to the space we have just moved through nor the space to which we are moving yet part of both.

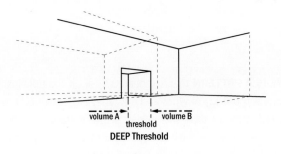

DEEP Threshold

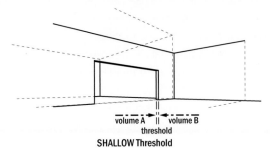

SHALLOW Threshold

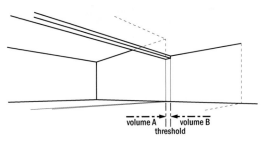

IMPLIED Threshold

TYPE

A TYPE IS A PATTERN that is repeated through multiple instances. Typology is the study of types and how they are organized based on the classification of their shared patterns. The standard typological pattern in architecture is usually at the room or building scale. When we call a building or room by a particular name or consider it as part of a larger category (i.e. hospital, elementary school, gallery, bedroom or residence), this is possible due to it being a type. The typological information is the fundamental characteristics of something that sets its basic identity and allows it to be understood as part of a larger group. While the idea of type and typology is a standard classification tool found in many different disciplines and applications in human thinking, an architectural type refers specifically to the event-to-form relationship that defines the composition of a space. The term *event-to-form* simply means that the activities that occur in a space can be represented by the formal composition of that space. At the room scale, type refers to the pattern between volume, circulation, formal elements and convexities based on the events that are present. At the building scale, type refers to the relationship between program volumes, their arrangement, massing and distribution in space. While a general pattern might be based on either formal or event information (see *Pattern*), a type or typological pattern always represents event information *through* formal composition. This allows a designer to work with spatial composition and materiality by assuming that the support for socio-cultural events is embedded in the arrangement of form and basic spatial qualities.

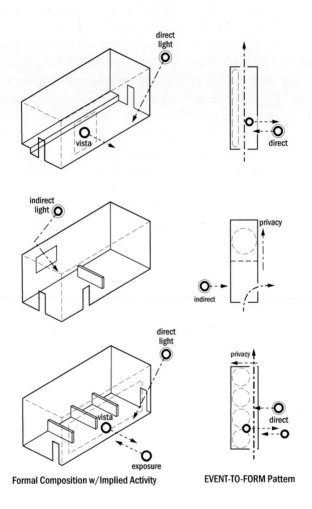

direct light

vista

direct

indirect light

privacy

indirect

direct light

vista

exposure

privacy

direct

Formal Composition w/Implied Activity

EVENT-TO-FORM Pattern

The compositional characteristics and spatial qualities of any space suggests the possibilities, success and limits of what human events are present (see *Convexity*, *Privacy*, *Connectedness* and *Force*). Spaces that are long and narrow with circulation through the centre axis support some events well but deny the possibility of others. If we make a formal change such as opening one wall to visual exposure and light, we change the events that are possible or easily supported. If the long space is then subdivided into smaller spaces, there is another immediate change in the possible events. In each of these cases, the change in possible event can be understood through the changes in formal composition. That composition can be reduced to basic patterns that describe only the fundamental characteristics of what makes up the identity of those spaces. If the events are common or codified in some way (through ritual, norms, policy or habit) so to be repeated, then the formal pattern can be applied in a new situation that involve the same events. At this point, a pattern becomes a type.

Since type is based on repetition, it requires the presence of things that already exist to be the basis of a new design proposal. However, the new design is not an exact duplication of the previous. Rather, each instance of a type must only meet the basic event-to-form patterns to be a member of that category. Once the basic patterns have been met, the new instance of the type can vary all other aspects of the formal design based on contextual needs (see *Pattern Mapping*). This means that several instances of the same type can look very different to each other while still satisfying the basic typological rules (i.e. type is not style). Where style focuses on classification through visual features, surface characteristic and features, type is always focused on underlying patterns of formal composition that imply socio-cultural use.

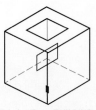

Existing Form (BUILDING)

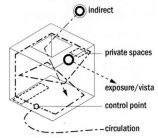

- indirect
- private spaces
- exposure/vista
- control point
- circulation

EVENT-TO-FORM Patterns

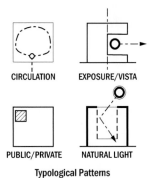

CIRCULATION   EXPOSURE/VISTA

PUBLIC/PRIVATE   NATURAL LIGHT

Typological Patterns

VISTA

A VISTA IS A VIEW from a space framed by an opening. It produces a scene or prospect which becomes an extension of the space from which it is seen. A vista is not simply any view – placing a window in a wall does not necessarily create a vista. Rather, the content of the vista must add quality to the space from which it is viewed through its presence and composition (see *Spatial Quality*). This means that what is being looked at is required to have some positive interpretation and value by the occupants of that space. The idea is similar to exposure although it operates in the opposite direction (see *Exposure*). Where exposure is the visibility of significant inside event from outside that space, vista is the visibility of significant outside event from inside that space.

While the standard use of the term vista implies something being seen at a great distance, this is not necessary when using the idea in architectural design. The only requirements are that the thing viewed is not within the space from which it is being seen, that it adds an essential quality to that space and the formal composition of the space frames the view in order to integrate it (i.e. creates a relationship). This means that a nearby natural element, such as a signature tree or rock, can be used as just as easily as a significant cultural building, skyline or mountain range. In all cases, vista is introduced into the space through either allowing the scene to replace one of the walls by creating a virtual edge or by framing a smaller focal through carefully placed openings, reinforcing the wall.

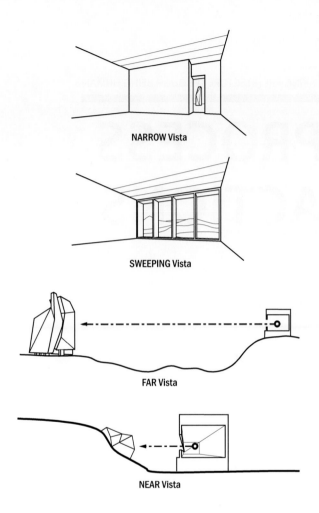

NARROW Vista

SWEEPING Vista

FAR Vista

NEAR Vista

MAKING ARCHITECTURE THROUGH BEING HUMAN

PROCESS ACTIONS

ONE OF THE THINGS THAT makes humans particularly human is the ability to think about a future state that does not yet exist, determine possible variations that could achieve that state and then deploy a strategy to make that future become real. This is design: the ability to explore, consider, analyse, propose, and, ultimately, bring something into being that is not currently present in the world. Architecture, as an act of design, imagines a future human environment that does not yet exist. To do this, architectural design uses several process actions as thinking tools. These tools help us organize our ideas, identify relevant content, analyse our context and manipulate formal and event information in larger relationships.

Process actions are not distinct from the other ideas, notions and concepts found in the previous sections. However, they focus on *how we do things* rather than how we interpret things. We use process actions in conjunction with the ideas found in the previous sections to achieve a particular outcome or to make a particular type of information visible (i.e. able to be used). For example, we use abstraction to understand hierarchy; assets and constraints are a fundamental way forces are resolved in design; coherence and cohesiveness are the basis of ordering systems by organizing elements and layers into a larger, integrated experience; extrapolation structures a chain of logic into the future while speculation suspends logic to imagine things that might be desirable; metaphor engages use and identity through connecting content between domains of knowledge; and pattern mapping uses knowledge of one space to organize the qualities of another.

ABSTRACTION

ABSTRACTION IS THE PROCESS of defining something (i.e. an object, space or environment for architecture) through its underlying purpose, defining characteristics, most basic operations or fundamental principles. It is a reduction of information that abandons all non-essential factors to focus on how something works, what events it causes to happen or what effect it might have. While the original thing might be very complex and have many interrelated parts, layers, or even random events associated with it, abstraction allows us to see past that complexity. As part of architectural design, abstraction allows us to identify things that matter in order to define goals or design questions. We then use that information to guide the arrangement of form into compositions that will have a high degree of relevance to its context. Abstraction is also a key tool in innovation as the ability to abstract a situation can allow us to produce novel outcomes while still conforming to essential needs.

The process of abstraction moves from objects to events to bring clarity to a complex, dynamic environment and identify critical factors for design. This can occur at two scales. *Granular abstraction* works by reducing an object through understanding the events associated with its parts. *Categorical abstraction* understands an object by identifying its essential characteristics that make it distinct from other things. It is categorical abstraction that we use to understand the relationship of a thing to larger hierarchies (see *Hierarchy*).

When we reduce something through *granular abstraction*, we move from a complex object to identify the parts that make up that

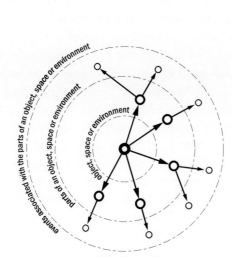

GRANULAR Abstraction

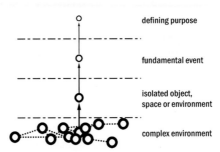

defining purpose

fundamental event

isolated object,
space or environment

complex environment

CATEGORICAL Abstraction

object. We can then consider the basic events associated with each part by asking what it does and what is the effect of its presence. The events become the focus of the design process and can be used to either refine the formal nature of that part or explore other ways of achieving the same effect. In both cases, the parts can be recompiled into a new whole (see *Coherence* and *Cohesiveness*). For example, if we think about an architectural element such as a stair, we can abstract that object into its parts and arrive with a list that will include tread, riser, nosing, railing, landing and stringer (at a basic level). Considering these elements, we can understand each through its abstracted purpose – a tread is for the placement of a foot, a riser to lift the body vertically, a nosing to protect the exposed edge of the tread and to improve safety by lengthening the tread and introducing friction, the railing to provide secondary support for balance, a landing to allow a person to rest and a stringer to physically support the diagonal movement of the treads. The clarification achieved through reduction allows us to ask a series of design questions such as: How long a tread should be in this context? How might the treads be supported? How might we provide friction to make the foot secure? What parts of the stair are directly engaged by the human body? How might we improve the durability of those parts? How can we provide secondary elements to improve mobility and balance of someone using the stair? These questions and the resulting design are all possible due to granular abstraction.

We can also abstract a thing using *categorical abstraction* by considering the thing as a whole rather than looking at it as an assembly of parts. When we use this form of abstraction, we work at a higher level of dimensionality and focus on a different type of information than when we use granular abstraction. Categorical abstraction ignores the parts to focus on the essential event that defines the nature of the thing (see *Identity*). This type of abstraction also allows us to abandon the physical nature of the thing to focus only on its effect – often allowing us to find another way to achieve that effect. In the case of a stair, the event associated with the whole is the efficient diagonal movement of a human body between two different vertical elevations through non-mechanized movement (i.e. the person uses their muscles). This is an abstraction because all non-necessary information has been removed leaving us with the essential nature of the stair. As a design tool, the categorical abstraction of a stair allows us to consider how a human might move vertically without being fixated on the normative object that we know as a stair. We can abandon all of the current parts of the stair as long as we satisfy the same events and defining nature of a stair.

Abstraction is a fundamental tool used in many situations in architectural design. It can be applied to all scales and types of information from entire buildings (what is the purpose or primary elements of the building?), building siting (what is important for the building to respond to in is context?), program (what are the essential activities that the building needs to contain?), program elements (what are the primary activities of a space?), architectural elements (what is the nature of stairs, doors, windows, or walls in this context?) and user events (what does this space need to support?). As a tool, abstraction makes basic questions, purposes, needs and operations visible and accessible to a design process.

ASSET-CONSTRAINT

ASSETS AND CONSTRAINTS ARE ways of organizing information in a design process. An asset is an opportunity that makes a design outcome easier, better or stronger while a constraint can be understood as a restriction that limits possibilities in the design. We can use assets and constraints to organize any information that affects an architectural design, ranging from non-formal events that affect formal design choices (see *Forces*) to existing qualities and formal relationships in our built environment (see *Importance*, *Proximity*, *Connectedness*, *Presence* and *Vista*).

We might be inclined to think about assets as positive and constraints as negative – however, this is not the case. Assets and constraints are both simply *useful* – they allow us to identify information that has a high degree of relevance to the design situation in a clear way. While any design situation contains a large amount of information, categorizing that information as either an asset or constraint allows a designer to focus on exploiting opportunities (assets) and accept or attempt to bypass, modify or diminish any restrictions (constraints) that might be present. The ultimate goal is to use this action to make clear decisions in a design project. Thinking about things as either an asset or a constraint allows us to consider how those things might directly affect the selection, placement and relationship between architectural forms and their context.

An *asset* is any formal element or event that makes something possible as it *creates an opportunity to achieve a desired outcome*. In this context, possible means that the presence of this element or event

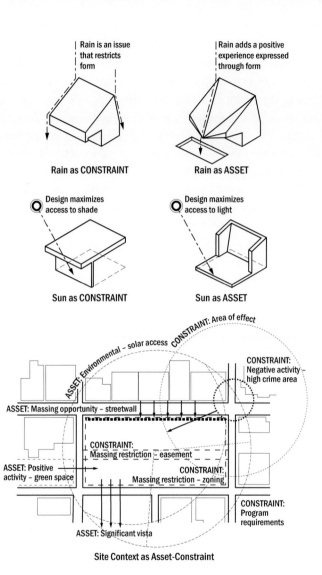

Rain is an issue that restricts form

Rain as CONSTRAINT

Rain adds a positive experience expressed through form

Rain as ASSET

Design maximizes access to shade

Sun as CONSTRAINT

Design maximizes access to light

Sun as ASSET

ASSET: Environmental – solar access

CONSTRAINT: Area of effect

CONSTRAINT: Negative activity – high crime area

ASSET: Massing opportunity – streetwall

CONSTRAINT: Massing restriction – easement

ASSET: Positive activity – green space

CONSTRAINT: Massing restriction – zoning

CONSTRAINT: Program requirements

ASSET: Significant vista

Site Context as Asset-Constraint

brings value into the proposed architectural environment. It does this by identifying and leveraging things that are already available in that context to integrate with the design proposal or by associating parts of the proposal with each other (see *Event Affinity*). An asset can range from the physical to the highly abstract. A good view is an asset if the type of activity that takes place in that room would benefit from a good view and the view is available. The presence of a defined street-wall is an asset if it allows for the strong identification of front in a building that needs it. The natural thermal resistance of a material is an asset if resistance to the transfer of heat or cold is a positive effect for the design purpose. The low cost of a material is an asset if that material satisfies a material need in a design. The speed of assembly of a structural system is an asset if the overall architectural outcome can benefit from decreased construction time (i.e. the benefit needs to be architectural and not just financial). Assets are things that allow us to do something more easily by linking one part of the proposed architectural composition with another or elements in its context.

A *constraint* is any formal element or event that restricts possibilities in a design situation. Restrict, in this situation, is not bad but *the creation of a boundary* to allow us to make decisions. In architectural design, precipitation as an event is a constraint as leaving a building open to rain will make it unusable. It is also a constraint because it restricts form to those shapes and slopes which will allow water to flow away from the habitable spaces. The activity that will take place in a space is also a constraint as it will limit the possibilities of formal composition and materiality. Zoning is a constraint as it will limit the possible height and massing of buildings as well as enforce required setbacks which restricts options for the architectural designer. A structurally weak material is a constraint if that material must be used but the design situation requires strength in the location it is needed.

Constraints create limits that help focus the formal composition of an architectural design proposal. This is a good thing.

An element or event in a design project can be both an asset and a constraint. Something that is an asset for one part of the proposal might be a constraint for another part of the same proposal, or events might change through time or cycles. Sunlight, for example, can be something beneficial to the experience of the spatial quality or an issue that is restrictive; or both at the same time. If we consider sunlight on a cold winter day, it would be an asset as its direct entry into a built space introduces light and heat that increase the experiential quality of that space. However, there are situations when too much light (glare) or the introduction of solar heat is not desired and, in these cases, sunlight would be considered a constraint as it will decrease the experience of the space. If we consider sunlight striking a building on a hot summer day, a designer would propose a form and materiality that would limit the direct entry light into the enclosed space so to minimalize the heat gain when cooling is required. In climates with seasonal shifts throughout the year (hot summers and cold winters), sunlight can change from being an asset to a constraint depending on the season. When phenomena are considered through assets and constraints, the physical nature of our environment can respond directly.

Assets and constraints are useful because they allow a designer to identify important aspects of an existing context as an integral part of a design process and provide limitations to focus the scope of the project. It would be difficult to make design decisions that are highly relevant without these ideas.

COHERENCE

COHERENCE IS WHEN SEVERAL elements in an environment or situation focus or align with a single objective, goal or focus. This is an important action in any human experience as it is the process that people use to create a whole out of parts, identify intentionality and generate large scale meaning. It is one of the ways we make things make sense. While coherence can operate at several dimensions from abstract ideas to visual communication, it is important in architectural design that coherence exists between formal elements, their properties, their spatial relationships and supported events.

As a process action, coherence is important for both the creation and interpretation of architectural design. It allows intentions to be recognized by organizing the relationship and hierarchy between various parts of a built environment towards a larger goal. This is an act of indicating meaning. It also is one of the ways quality is judged. As coherence is a positive experience for humans, we naturally consider something that is coherent as good. So, when the elements in a designed environmental create a strong relationship towards an overall purpose by reinforcing each other, we consider this to be "good design".

Coherence is created through *reinforcement*. Reinforcement is a type of repetition where more than one thing is performing the same action or is aligned to the same event, idea or principle. This repetition is not physical but conceptual. When we find several elements in the built environment supporting the same idea (i.e. there is redundancy), that idea is interpreted as both intentional and important (see

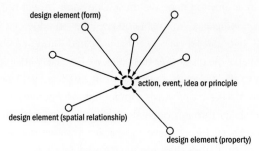

design element (form)

action, event, idea or principle

design element (spatial relationship)

design element (property)

Conceptual Structure (REINFORCEMENT)

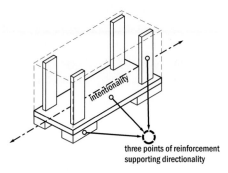

Intentionality

three points of reinforcement
supporting directionality

PHYSICAL Manifestation

Repetition and *Importance*). A common example is an ordering principle. When we select an axis as an ordering principle to organize a spatial experience, this is simply an idea. In order to make that idea present in an environment, we must align some aspect of the built space to *indicate* axis. We might choose either an edge of a series of buildings, two parallel walls or a line indicated through a change in the material of the ground. At this point, we have allowed an ordering principle to affect formal composition, but we do not yet have coherence. If we believe that the axis is important as it operates to produce spatial legibility through orientation, directionality and other interpretative effects, we will have to indicate this importance through reinforcement. Rather than just one element making the axis, we would involve others – this might be adding parallel walls, a mark on the ground, a focal element at the termination point of the axis, a change in height or massing of the edges to indicate importance and so on. The more things in the environment that support the axis, the stronger the axis becomes as an experience as it is understood as hierarchically important and clearly intentional through coherence.

Coherence can be found at different levels of hierarchy and with varying layers of interaction. Simple coherence might involve a rectangular slab, a rectangular footer and a rectangular column which all have their long side facing the same way. This produces a three-element coherent system which indicates intentionality. Other systems might involve tens or hundreds of elements in an ordered relationship. The important aspect is that all the elements are *aligned* to work together towards a single goal. Coherence can be used to organize single elements with each other or larger groups integrated into other types of systems (see *Cohesiveness*).

COHESIVENESS

COHESIVENESS IS WHEN ONE ELEMENT works in multiple ways to achieve several objectives at the same time. The action produces an economy in a design situation as instead of a separate element for each purpose or need, one thing can support many actions, events, ideas or principles. Cohesive elements become important due to this relationship – not through repetition or attention but through performative relationship. If we were to remove a cohesive element, the overall design would be weakened by several factors, the spatial quality would be reduced, many relationships would be broken and several new elements would have to be introduced to achieve the same goals but making the environment less resolved. In architectural design, an element is usually an object or surface, its properties and the space it defines. The goal of cohesiveness is to allow a single thing to have the largest effect possible by making it do as much as it can in the simplest way. Where coherence is about the relationship of the whole to the parts, cohesiveness is about the relationship of a part to other parts – either physical or imagined (see *Objectification*).

Cohesiveness is created through *efficiency*. Efficiency means that something is done with the minimum of effort to achieve the maximum effect. An effect in architectural design is how an object or surface engages with human needs through environmental, ergonomic, social or cultural information (see *Dimensionality*). For an object or surface to be efficient in an architectural environment, it needs to perform as many different purposes as possible. If we have a door located in a wall within a building and a lower ceiling over the door (bulkhead), each one of these elements will start with a single architectural purpose. The wall is to create an edge, the door is to provide passage of a body and the bulkhead to identify the door location. However, the bulkhead can be shaped in such a way to respond to more events and have a greater effect without adding more things to the space. If the bulkhead is elongated, thinned and constructed of a white or reflective surface material, it could also act as a light shelf to bounce light deeper into the volume; create containment to make a threshold space that conceptually separates the door from the corridor; guide circulation by suggesting directionality through implied motion; and identify an important part of the environment through difference. In this way, the bulkhead, as a single design element, operates to satisfy several different spatial and social needs at the same time. The multiple uses of this one element may be said to be an example of efficiency and that the element is highly cohesive to the environment in which it exists (i.e. cannot be removed easily without negative effects or loss of quality).

We can understand cohesiveness to be an important aspect in refining a formal environment. Refinement is the process of making something better through small changes that strengthen existing relationships or overall intentions. Any aspect of the built environment can be refined by increasing the cohesiveness of existing or proposed elements. Since cohesiveness stresses the multiple uses of a single element, the result is usually a less complicated design proposal with stronger part-to-part relationships but clear and relevant intentionality.

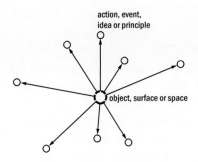

Conceptual Structure (EFFICIENCY)

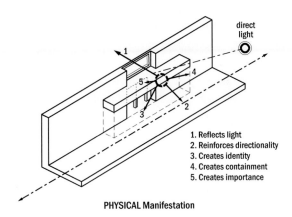

1. Reflects light
2. Reinforces directionality
3. Creates identity
4. Creates containment
5. Creates importance

PHYSICAL Manifestation

EXTRAPOLATION

ONE OF THE ABILITIES that makes humans particularly human is our ability to extend our thoughts into a future that does not yet exist and then adjust our actions to respond to that condition. Extrapolation is the act of predicting a future or end condition based on assuming that current trends will continue without a significant disruption. It starts with understanding what we have or what we know and then asks the question: "Where does it go?". Design actions are future orientated as designers are focused on things that do not yet exist but they can imagine coming into being. While it is easy to think about the start of a new pattern (prototype) or something unique or novel to a situation as being future-orientated, even a new instance of a repeated and well-known pattern (see *Type*) does not yet exist until it is proposed. A design proposal is an argument for something that *should* exist, something that *will* support our needs (which include desires and beliefs), and something that *might* come into the world. Extrapolation is one way of determining that future condition through isolating current events or needs and extending them forward in time to a logical outcome. It always moves from a known present to an unknown but predictable future.

In architectural design, extrapolation can range from small predictions that we take for granted to the generation of imaginative and extreme proposals that are still extensions of logic. It occurs every time we ask how someone might use a space that has not yet been designed or built, how a space might adapt to future activities or what types of buildings might we have in the future based on current

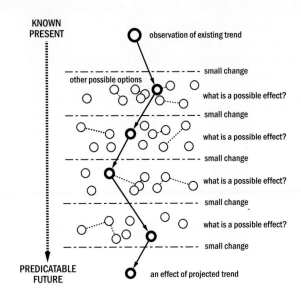

KNOWN
PRESENT

observation of existing trend

small change

other possible options

what is a possible effect?

small change

what is a possible effect?

small change

what is a possible effect?

small change

what is a possible effect?

small change

PREDICATABLE
FUTURE

an effect of projected trend

trends in, for example, energy production, resource management, material science, social structures or cultural values. The process is the same although content and focus will change the starting information and when the extrapolation stops.

Extrapolation operates through a chain of logical assumptions using the question: "What might be the effect if …?" in an iterative process. Iteration is the repetition of the same action over and over but making small changes at each pass to generate a small improvement with the intention of producing a stronger outcome overall. Extrapolation uses iteration to return either practical information for direct use in a project or to forecast the nature of our future built environment but without immediate application. The action begins always with an observation of an existing trend – for architecture, this is something that will have a formal effect or can be spatialized in some way. If we look at trends in housing and see that more people were either single or living as couples without children, we could extrapolate the future effect on architecture. The iterative process could start by asking what might be the lifestyle changes that would affect spatial design; move to questions of changes in adjacency needs; then question the needed scale and composition of houses; consider a new normative housing composition; theorize the formal effect of childless families; move into questions of co-habitation or community development; predict the radical shift of housing stock; and so on. At any point, the questions can branch to create a new thread and the process can also stop at any point if it returns something usable or interesting for the designer's context.

Extrapolation is one way to use current knowledge from our actions in space – facts, observations, activities and values – to consider the shape of our future built environment.

METAPHOR

A METAPHOR IS WHEN one thing is used to understand something else but those two things exist in different and separate domains of knowledge. While we have a tradition of defining metaphor as a linguistic expression or a figure of speech, it is really a conceptual process – one of the core mental structures of how humans think. Metaphors allow us to understand new experiences or intangible ideas by associating them with things we already know. If we consider people walking as the movement of water, we have created a metaphor. This might have the linguistic expression of "crowds are rivers" or "circulation moves like a stream" but under these expressions is the conceptual metaphor HUMAN MOVEMENT IS WATER MOVEMENT. It is a metaphor because people walking is in the knowledge domain of human locomotion while movement of water belongs to the knowledge domain of liquid dynamics. Domains are conceptual containers that allow us to group related ideas together (see *Containment*). The creation of a boundary around these ideas identifies a shared purpose between all the elements found within that boundary while also reinforcing a particular point of view and responsibility toward that contained knowledge. When there is value to relate one type of information to another type of information in different domains of activity or knowledge, we use a metaphor. The key to identifying a metaphor is that the relationship generated includes incongruence – we describe one thing as something that it is obviously not. In the example above, people are not water molecules and there is no situation where people could *literally* be water. However, while metaphors are incongruent, they are also very useful because they allow us to consider the target information in a new way or allow us to transfer meaning through the association, especially if it is based on embodied knowledge.

There are three major categories of metaphors. Each is used in a different way by architectural designers, have different scales and different effects. The categories are image metaphors, relational metaphors and correlational metaphors. The first two metaphor types are based on how one thing resembles another thing – either through visual elements and characteristics (image) or how the elements are organized (relations). The third type of metaphor is based on a relationship that has developed through the interaction of our bodies and each other in an environment where we use that information to understand more abstract ideas (correlation).

Image metaphors associate the visual information of an architectural form with some other visual information from another domain of knowledge. The main operation of these metaphors is through the creation of a relationship based on similarity – what something looks like and how much it resembles something else. When we call a building a cloud, a gherkin, a sunflower, a shell or a bird's nest based on how it looks, this is an image metaphor. The building is none of these things but produces a relationship between the buildings and domains of atmospheric phenomena, plants, zoology or animal artefacts (in these examples) in order to generate some additional and, hopefully, positive value. The most common version of this metaphor in architectural design is found at a large scale – using the shape of something to either affect the shape of the overall building or as an ordering principle to arrange formal elements. In this way, the metaphor is used as a guide to align all the many parts and other aspects of the design (see *Coherence*).

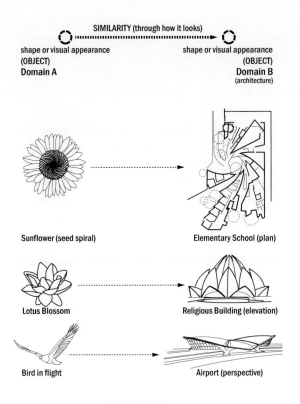

SIMILARITY (through how it looks)

shape or visual appearance
(OBJECT)
Domain A

shape or visual appearance
(OBJECT)
Domain B
(architecture)

Sunflower (seed spiral)

Elementary School (plan)

Lotus Blossom

Religious Building (elevation)

Bird in flight

Airport (perspective)

IMAGE Metaphor

The second type of metaphor that uses similarity information is relational metaphor. These metaphors differ significantly from image metaphor as relational metaphors focus on performative information – what something does or how it works rather what it looks like. If we use a shell as source material for a design project through image metaphor, we would map the unique shape and visual attributes of a shell such as a gentle arc, a bi-directional curve and a smooth surface. We might even make the form white to associate it more strongly with the source material. However, if we were to transfer relational information, we abandon what something looks like and instead focus on how it performs through the relationship between its parts. We would understand the shell as being a thin membrane between interior and exterior that is an exoskeleton. This could produce several different architectural responses depending on our focus. The metaphor of the shell might change how we think about structure (moving from point loads to stress skins), circulation (a shell is not punctured so movement would stress slipping between shell parts) or environmental factors such as temperature and air movement between inside and outside. As an image metaphor, a sunflower would stress a radial ordering principle with a large core (disk florals) and multiple connections (the petals or ray florals) but as a relational metaphor, the focus would be on how the sunflower tracks the movement of light. A cloud as an image metaphor would translates as formal properties such as white, soft appearance and fluffiness but as a relational metaphor would address the absorption and expulsion of moisture. We find relational metaphors used in biomimicry in order to innovate successfully. A relational metaphor changes how we might understand the organization of parts and introduces a new structure that should be highly relevant but also not what we might expect.

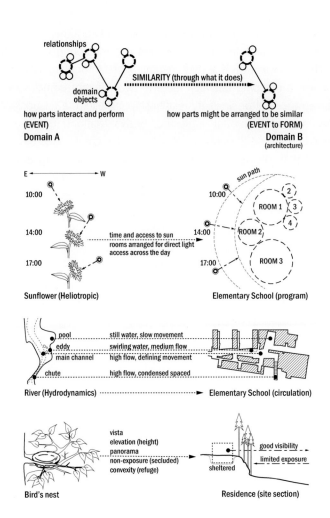

relationships

SIMILARITY (through what it does)

domain objects

how parts interact and perform
(EVENT)
Domain A

how parts might be arranged to be similar
(EVENT to FORM)
Domain B
(architecture)

E ←——→ W

10:00

14:00

17:00

time and access to sun
rooms arranged for direct light
access across the day

sun path

10:00

14:00

17:00

ROOM 1

2
3
4

ROOM 2

ROOM 3

Sunflower (Heliotropic)

Elementary School (program)

pool   still water, slow movement
eddy   swirling water, medium flow
main channel high flow, defining movement
chute   high flow, condensed spaced

River (Hydrodynamics) ·······························► Elementary School (circulation)

vista
elevation (height)
panorama
non-exposure (secluded)
convexity (refuge)

good visibility

limited exposure

sheltered

Bird's nest

Residence (site section)

RELATIONAL Metaphor

Correlational metaphors are very different to either image or relational metaphors. In fact, we use these metaphors constantly with little awareness that they are metaphors. A correlational metaphor is a mapping between ideas in two different domains that have no causal or similarity relationship. Instead, the relationship becomes fixed through either our body's relationship with our environment or through social and cultural agreements (i.e. we agree that this thing is related to this other thing). Correlational metaphors are based on our experience in the world and we use that experience to give meaning to more abstract ideas. When we make centres important, allow object to feel like they move when they do not, give shapes personalities or interpret closeness as an emotional relationship, we are using correlational metaphors (see *Identity*, *Implied Stability*, *Implied Motion*, *Implied Action*, *Importance*, *Personification* and *Relationship*). We also create correlational metaphors when we agree that non-visual information from another domain is associated with visual information expressed through architectural content. If marble is identified with social status or columns and pediments associated with a political system, this is a correlational relationship between two different domains of knowledge (social relations > architecture, politics > architecture). It is the correlational metaphor that allows social and cultural information to have an effect on architectural forms by assigning it meaning based on what we agree it means.

The difficulty in metaphor use is always in the selection and translation of the source material – an irrelevant source will produce an irrelevant design. We must always figure out why we are using the non-architectural content and what value is returned by the metaphor.

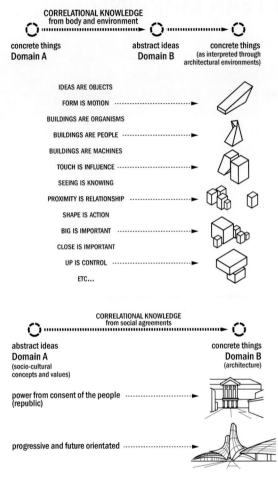

CORRELATIONAL KNOWLEDGE
from body and environment

concrete things
Domain A

abstract ideas
Domain B

concrete things
(as interpreted through
architectural environments)

IDEAS ARE OBJECTS

FORM IS MOTION

BUILDINGS ARE ORGANISMS

BUILDINGS ARE PEOPLE

BUILDINGS ARE MACHINES

TOUCH IS INFLUENCE

SEEING IS KNOWING

PROXIMITY IS RELATIONSHIP

SHAPE IS ACTION

BIG IS IMPORTANT

CLOSE IS IMPORTANT

UP IS CONTROL

ETC...

CORRELATIONAL KNOWLEDGE
from social agreements

abstract ideas
Domain A
(socio-cultural
concepts and values)

concrete things
Domain B
(architecture)

power from consent of the people
(republic)

progressive and future orientated

CORRELATIONAL Metaphor

PATTERN MAPPING

PATTERN MAPPING IS THE USE of one space to design another space through the transfer of underlying patterns that define spatial and experiential qualities. A mapping is a tool that associates two sets of elements where the structure and relations of the elements in one set are used to arrange the structure and relations of the elements in the second set. In architecture, a space (i.e. a formal environment) is a set of elements. We experience a space as a defined volume which includes fixed surfaces, material properties, assemblies, relational adjacencies and compositional arrangements. Each of these – objects, properties, their relationships and spatial qualities – are an element in the set. The set will also include socio-spatial events such as connectedness, exposure, privacy and vista as these are extensions of the physical environment. Since the physical composition of a space can reflect the events that occur in that space (see *Pattern*), the focus of pattern mapping is proposing the composition of new spaces based on transferring the pattern of related or similar events from existing spaces. This allows the transfer of the underlying principles while remaining flexible to how that pattern is resolved in the formal composition. The result of a pattern mapping *does not need to look like* the original space but, rather, *needs to perform like* the original space.

A room, building or some other formal arrangement in our built environment might be thought of simply as walls, floors and ceilings. However, these physical elements produce unique compositions that are not arbitrary. Rather, their arrangement supports human events and experiences that are not physical objects – such as privacy,

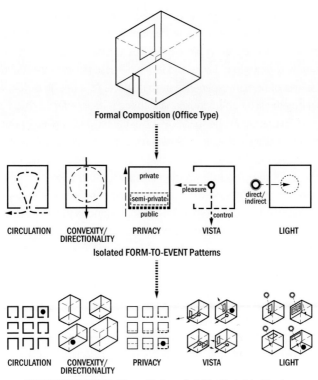

Formal Composition (Office Type)

CIRCULATION   CONVEXITY/   PRIVACY   VISTA   LIGHT
               DIRECTIONALITY

private

pleasure

semi-private

public   control

direct/
indirect

Isolated FORM-TO-EVENT Patterns

CIRCULATION   CONVEXITY/   PRIVACY   VISTA   LIGHT
               DIRECTIONALITY

POSSIBLE VARIATIONS of Formal Patterns Satisfying Underlying Events

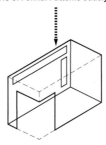

MAPPED PATTERNS to New Formal Composition

visibility, circulation, exposure and vista. These human events are made possible by the unique composition and materiality of the physical space and each event produces a pattern. Our built environment is composed of layers and layers of these patterns that defines qualities of human experience in that space. As a design action, we can isolate each pattern individually to focus on its effect. In this way, a pattern present in one space can be extracted and applied to a new situation if there is relevance between that pattern and the new architectural space. Relevance means that there is alignment between the content of the pattern from the first space and the needs, use and operation of the new space. If a vista would benefit a new space, we can map the formal pattern of a space that supports the event of view as a basis of the new formal composition. However, it would make little sense to transfer a pattern based on public exposure if the new space requires privacy as there is a conflict of needs.

Pattern mapping is used every time a named space or building category is designed (i.e. "bedroom", "office", "single-family house", "library", "museum" or "restaurant"). In these cases, the name refers to a room or building *type* – which is simply a collection of patterns that becomes repeated through being successful (see *Type* and *Program*). For example, when a new office is designed, we use our knowledge of the patterns that make offices successful – the particular arrangement of distance between walls, source of light, volume of space, number of entrances and location of access which support events such as privateness, connectedness, illumination, exposure, oversight and social status. We do this by mapping the successful formal and event patterns from the existing space as the basis of the design of the new space.

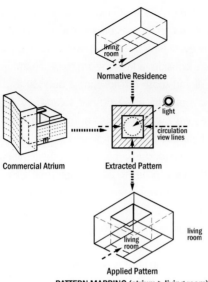

living room

Normative Residence

Commercial Atrium

light

circulation
view lines

Extracted Pattern

living
room

living
room

Applied Pattern

PATTERN MAPPING (atrium > living room)

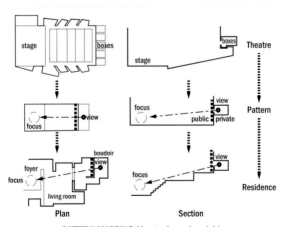

stage

boxes

stage

boxes

Theatre

focus

view

focus

view

Pattern

public   private

boudoir

foyer

view

focus

focus

view

Residence

living room

Plan

Section

PATTERN MAPPING (theatre box > boudoir)

It is also possible to map patterns between spaces or buildings that are very different. This action focuses on a small number of patterns that have a strong relevance for the new space and can be a form of innovation. When we consider a living room to be an atrium, a restaurant as either a dining room or museum, a boudoir as a theatre box or a library as a retail space, we do not mean they are literally these spaces. Rather, we mean there is an important event in the second space which can be used in improve the quality of the first space. The event is understood as a pattern and then the pattern is mapped between the two spaces to arrange a formal response. For example, an atrium is a large, convex, well-connected, and public open space usually found in the centre of a commercial building with a deep floorplate. Its quality is one of openness and light achieved through being exposed to the sky (no roof or extensive skylights). If we consider a living room as an atrium, we do not mean that we make it commercial, unproportionally large or public. Rather, the relevant patterns to inform a residential design are considering the relationship between solid and void within the overall building massing, the relationship to light entering the building and the relationship to circulation. Each relationship is a pattern that can be mapped to the residence without bringing any of the other content of the atrium.

We can also innovate through pattern mapping to produce new types of spaces or new experiences. A boudoir is a small space off a bedroom that holds a dressing table for personal grooming. It is highly private and usually isolated from the rest of the house. However, if we use a mapping between a theatre box and the boudoir, it introduces novel but relevant information to change the standard arrangement of spaces. A theatre box is also a private space but has a key difference to the boudoir – rather than being fully isolated, the dominate pattern is one of directionality of view with a clear line of sight to a stage while shielding the occupants from a return view. The view event of the theatre box does not traditionally exist in the context of the boudoir. However, there is relevance to give the individual in the boudoir the ability to oversee more public aspects of the house without being seen themselves, an idea that can be supported by spatial composition. The more public and active parts of the house would be mapped to the idea of a stage – this might be the entrance or maybe the living room – and the pattern would allow or shield view depending on the location of the occupant.

What makes pattern mapping particularly useful for architecture is the lack of need of translation. It is not a metaphor but a type of intra-domain mapping where information is transferred directly between elements in the same domain of knowledge (i.e. architecture). Since the information is already in an architectural form – i.e. it is spatialized and describes the properties and relationship of physical elements to social needs – the mapping requires only a consideration of application. In the boudoir/theatre box example, the way that privacy and view works in the boudoir is *exactly the same* as the way privacy and view works in the theatre box. While the rooms are different, the underlying patterns are the same. Metaphor, in contrast, requires active translation as information is moving across domain boundaries (see *Metaphor*).

SPECULATION

SPECULATION IS THE ACT OF FORMING a theory without facts, proof or firm evidence. In design, it is used to make a proposal based on loosely connected ideas, desires, opinions and known things without being concerned if those relationships are defensible or even real. Unlike other future-orientated actions (see *Extrapolation*), speculation does not start with current conditions, mapping existing trends or identifying real needs. Rather, it is a product of wishful thinking – the act of making something up that we want to be real even though we know it is not. The purpose of speculation in architectural design is to shift our cultural values and goals, remove our biases or suspend pre-determined outcomes. As such, speculative outcomes are focused on presenting ideas through architectural content that will change how someone sees the world and how we define ourselves (see *Identity*). Speculation produces the intention: *this is where we want to go, how do we get there?*

Speculation operates through imagining a potential future condition without any concern for the known present. The result is an aspirational fiction that uses architectural content to explore larger socio-cultural and technological ideas. It is only after the future state has been proposed do we worry about how we can convince others that it *might be possible*. Possible in this case does not mean real, logical, or predictable. It means plausible – as in someone will see it as believable. There are two important factors in plausibility. First is to link the future condition with some aspect of the present so that it suggests a possible path of development from our current context

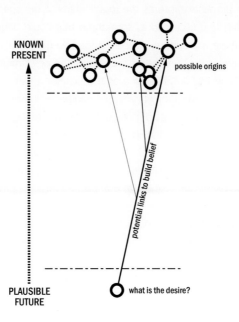

KNOWN
PRESENT

possible origins

potential links to build belief

PLAUSIBLE
FUTURE

what is the desire?

to how that fictional position might have occurred. This link is gestural as a loose association rather than a fixed causation. Second is to connect the project outcomes to a desire in the viewer by relating it to things people already care about, crave or fancy – things that are interesting. People do not believe in things that are factual, they believe in things they *want* to believe in. In the case of speculation, when the proposal captures the imagination of the spectator, it is more likely to be accepted as something that could happen. If, for example, there is a cultural concern about overpopulation and lack of living spaces for humans, an architectural project might take on this idea in several ways as long as the position can be spatialized and related to form. Projects might imagine buildings populating locations that are currently out of reach such as orbiting in our lower atmosphere or terraforming locations with extreme climates using buildings to produce microclimates for human habitation. Either of these ideas can be speculated using architectural knowledge and representational tools to visualize that future. Once the project direction has been set, the details can be flushed out to build a back story in order to make it more believable. Orbiting buildings could identify something interesting in the physics of space travel. The microclimate buildings could connect to larger scale climatic phenomena about thermodynamics such as lake-effect or heat islands. These ideas would be engaged through architectural forms.

Speculation is not concerned with logic and moves from a desired future to a known present. It works in a top-down approach tying all details to the project focus (see *Coherence*). It is not used to develop core architectural knowledge but instead uses architectural ideas to address socio-cultural ideas. The purpose of speculation is not to generate a real architecture project but encourages discussion around ideas that can be visualized through architectural content.